The Magic of Birds

What People Are Saying About

The Magic of Birds

What a delightful journey into the magical world of birds! The author swoops through a whole flock of different bird types, their meanings, myths and magic. From songbirds to water birds and all kinds of feathered wonders, it is an absolute avian treasure trove.

Rachel Patterson, English witch, podcast host, and bestselling author of over 30 books, including *Pagan Portals - Animal Magic*, the *Kitchen Witchcraft* series, and *Beneath the Moon*

The Magic of Birds is an intriguing exploration of the symbolism and power of the birds all around us. The writing style is straightforward, and the text is easy to navigate, making it ideal as a reference to look up specifics but also a fun book to read from start to finish. Offering everything from stories and rituals to folklore and magical correspondences, there's something here for any reader.

Morgan Daimler, author of *Celtic Fairies in North America*

The Magic of Birds by Mabh Savage is a book I didn't know I needed to read. Not only did I learn about songbirds, birds of prey, carrion eaters, and more, but also, I learned specific ways to enhance my magickal practice with birds. Carefully researched and very detailed, *The Magic of Birds* includes folklore, poetry, and rituals that call the reader into a deeper relationship with the natural world. I feel nourished by Mabh Savage's words and know other readers will too!

Irisanya Moon, author of *Circe: Goddess of Sorcery, Hestia: Goddess of Hearth, Home and Community*, and many other Moon Books titles

The Magic of Birds

Mabh Savage

MOON BOOKS

London, UK
Washington, DC, USA

CollectiveInk

First published by Moon Books, 2025
Moon Books is an imprint of Collective Ink Ltd.,
Unit 11, Shepperton House, 89 Shepperton Road, London, N1 3DF
office@collectiveinkbooks.com
www.collectiveinkbooks.com
www.moon-books.net

For distributor details and how to order please visit the 'Ordering' section on our website.

Text copyright: Mabh Savage 2024

ISBN: 978 1 80341 060 9
978 1 80341 061 6 (ebook)
Library of Congress Control Number: 2024940334

A CIP catalogue record for this book is available from the British Library.

Design: Lapiz Digital Services
Illustrated by Kay Savage

UK: Printed and bound by CPI Group (UK) Ltd, Croydon, CR0 4YY
US: Printed and bound by Thomson-Shore, 7300 West Joy Road, Dexter, MI 48130

We operate a distinctive and ethical publishing philosophy in
all areas of our business, from our global network of authors to
production and worldwide distribution.

Contents

For Loki, Lopt, Loptr, Lopt-Eldr, sky fire, sky treader; you who wear the Falcon Cloak and remind us that "human" is not the only shape – and certainly not the most superior one.

About the Author

Mabh Savage is a pagan author and musician with a particular interest in the magic of animals and plants. As well as having a lifelong fascination for Irish legends, Paganism, and spirituality, she's also a member of the global Covenant of Hekate and has assisted in some fascinating collaborative projects such as working with members all over the world to create a song for Hekate (Mother of Dreams, available on Mabh's SoundCloud, https://soundcloud.com/mabh-savage).

Mabh is the secretary of the Pagan Federation Children and Families Team which aims to make life easier for Pagan families in Great Britain. She's also the current editor of *Aether*, the magazine for Pagan families.

She's been a member of the UK Green Party for many years, and believes firmly that it's possible to reverse the damage being done to our planet with the right focus and action now. Gaining a better understanding of our feathered cousins and other animals and fostering a closer connection to nature is just one vital step towards that.

www.mabhsavage.com
https://www.patreon.com/MabhSavage
https://www.facebook.com/MabhLSavage
https://twitter.com/Mabherick
https://www.instagram.com/mabherick/

Previous Books

A Modern Celt
ISBN: 978-1-78099-796-4

Pagan Portals: Celtic Witchcraft
ISBN: 978-1-78535-314-7

Practically Pagan: An Alternative Guide to Planet
Friendly Living
ISBN: 978-1-78904-445-4

Acknowledgments

Thank you, kids, for keeping me real and reminding me not to take myself so seriously. Thank you, spouse, for coping with my frequent bouts of hyperfocus and putting up with me answering questions like, "Where's the milk?" with responses along the lines of, "Did you know starlings migrate here from Russia?". Thank you, friends, who are still there when I disappear into my laptop for weeks on end! And finally, thank you, Kay, for your magnificent artwork and unending support.

Preface

I'm a writer, a musician, and a witch. Over the past few years, I have been writing a great deal about how Celtic and particularly Irish mythology and history influences me (*A Modern Celt, Moon Books, 2013; Pagan Portals: Celtic Witchcraft, Moon Books, 2016*) and, of course, how I work with this in my daily life. One day, it occurred to me that my greatest fascination, even wider and more encompassing than my passion for mythology, is how I am affected by nature. By 'nature' I mean everything from club moss to mountains. Voles to volcanoes. And of course, robins to rocs.

With this in mind, I set out to produce some volumes that will highlight how the natural world has not only influenced me, but the entirety of humanity, for many millennia. To do this, I decided to take an aspect of nature and really focus on it; what is magical about it, where it thrives, and who it affects. Then Moon Books announced they were doing a series exactly in this vein, and I was delighted to be able to contribute my musings on the *Magic of Birds*.

My initial goal was to separate the natural world into different types of animals with the goal of achieving something a little different from your standard reference book. I wanted to take a single category of creatures and examine their magical correspondences via folklore, history, and personal experience. I wish to empower you to dip your toe into the pool of wisdom, and see if the salmon tickle your feet!

With that in mind, the first category of nature that flowed from my fanciful pen was the birds. Why did I choose birds? The truth is… they told me to! Every day, in every way, they have been chirping, squawking, tweeting, and flapping their way around my brain until there had to be an outlet, and the inevitable vent was the volume you now hold.

Birds are all around us. In the densest, noisiest city, and the solemn, silent woods. By the lakes where the water's still and the crushing roar of the ocean. In the park over paths and picnic tables and over wild wastelands, thorny and desolate. I am fascinated by their ability to adapt to almost every part of our planet, a vital, mystical magic in and of itself.

Introduction

Today a magpie relieved itself on my windshield. I had mixed emotions; frustration at the slushy, yellowish splatter on the glass, and an immediate sense of gratitude, as bird poo is a good omen for travel. Although, on that note, when on holiday, don't believe anyone who tells you a bird has just pooped on you – it's a scam! Seriously, a couple of years ago, there seemed to be a spate of incidents in some parts of South America, where travellers were approached by 'helpful' strangers offering to wipe the offending bird poop off their back or hair: "Just take your bag off please and I'll help you out there." At which point the bag is snatched. Awful. Anyway, the origins of the bird poo myth seem lost in the mists of time, but I definitely remember my nana telling me I was lucky to have some guano on my suitcase, as bird poo meant a safe journey. *A Dictionary of Superstitions* (Opie; Tatem,1989) concurs that since at least 1878, there have been mentions of this odd belief: that bird faeces on one's luggage or even clothing will impart great fortune during any journey.

Today, I watched the double splat spread wetly over my windscreen with resignation. I opened my car door and there were four magpies in the hawthorn tree above and to the right of my parking space.

One for sorrow
Two for joy
Three for a girl
Four for a boy.

A boy, eh. I was already hanging out with my boy, the then six-year-old Nathan who was intrigued by the black and white mischiefs that mocked us from the branches above. The magpies told our tiny story through a folk rhyme, and I would like to tell theirs through this book. Not just the magpies' story, of course; the magical story of all the birds that have inspired clever rhymes, country customs and mystical myths and legends throughout the centuries.

Birds have appeared intertwined with human history since the Palaeolithic times. Some of the earliest known Oceanic sculptures are mortars and pestles from New Guinea decorated with birds and birds' heads. Freestanding figures which are presumed to be from a similar time period also show the features of birds. Whilst we can only guess at the true significance of these avian adornments, it's clear to see that, even hundreds of thousands of years ago, birds were important to humans; important enough to draw, sculpt, and tell tales of.

The aforementioned magpie rhyme itself is no recent addition to our bird folklore. In Britain, it is thought that this prophetic nursery rhyme dates back to at least the early sixteen-hundreds (Opie; Tatem, 1989). 400 plus years of using these black and white carrion eaters to tell us what might be around the corner. What other secrets might these feathered fates hold for us?

With that question in mind, let us walk through an exhibition of folklore, superstition, myth, legend, song, rhyme, and stories that all highlight the occult significance of birds. I want to show you how birds bring magic to our world, not just through their beauty and natural presence, but through mystical correspondences, associations with deities, and links to spirits and even other worlds. As part of the *"Magic of..."* series, this book is intended as an introduction only, however, I will cite sources wherever possible, so that you may research further to find your own answers and create your own wonderful connection to the magic of birds.

In Ancient Egypt, the ibis was a sacred animal; a symbol of Thoth, the god of knowledge and writing. As we start this journey of exploration together, I look to ibis-headed Thoth in the hope that you the reader, and I the writer, will both finish this book wealthier of the mind and the spirit. Ultimately, I want you to see all birds as magical creatures; symbols of sorcery and wonder. If you wish, you will be able to use the knowledge within this book to make your own magic, or at the very least, find your own spiritual connection to the birds of our world.

I will look at many different cultures, although my own passion is for local folklore and Celtic tales, so you may find a bias towards British and European superstitions and stories. I love to compare how each beast is seen through the eyes of differing religions and paths though, so I will take you with me to visit Africa, Australia, and even the New World on our exploration of the magic of birds. You may be surprised at the similarities, or the differences, in how birds are viewed in different parts of the world.

Some birds I'll say a lot about – these are my favourites and have either visited with me many times or have become a passion of mine for their folklore and magical associations. Because this is a short, introductory volume, for some birds I have listed just a few correspondences, associations, and folklore snippets. I hope that this inspires you to go out and find out more about these wonderful feathered beasts yourself.

I've also interspersed the information about birds with some poetry, all by myself unless otherwise stated. For me, writing poems is a truly magical way to connect to the world around me, particularly the natural world. And, unsurprisingly, birds have inspired so many poems throughout my life.

Above all, this is a book for pleasure. Birds are beautiful, mystical, and magical. Their tales are wondrous and mysterious, even humorous at times. Let the stories enchant and entice you; and if you find something that resonates with you while upon this journey, so much the better.

Chapter 1

Songbirds

There is something undeniably miraculous about birdsong. Nature's airs: sometimes light and bright, sometimes fast and vicious, other times lilting and melancholy, calling down the evening in staves of sheer beauty. I never tire of listening to the birds outside my home or in the nearby woods, particularly the blackbirds whose calls are some of the first I remember being to recognise without having to check with someone else. The blackbird has a flute-like run of notes, but also a shouting, scolding call when contesting local territory with other birds or, sometimes, humans that get too close. The wren, similarly, has a loud voice – one of the loudest in comparison to its diminutive size. The robin, too, is highly musical, trilling delightfully while I dig in the garden, then alighting on the handle of one of my tools to survey my work, before tucking into some of the grubs I've unearthed.

Thrushes are quite the international singers; a global hit, if you will. The African Thrush (Turdus Pelios) warbles a variety of refrains, including a sweet high-low riff that really catches the ear. In North America, the veery (*Catharus fuscescens*) calls its own name, trilling high yet heartily from the depths of the forest. *Birds & Blooms* (Roth, 2022) describes the veery's call as "going straight to the heart of the romantic listener." I love this, because that is exactly what birdsong does. It hits some essential part of the spirit, tapping into wells of nostalgia and gently urging you to stop, pause, listen, and absorb the moment; an accidental gift, perhaps, but a treasured gift, nonetheless. It's effortless to be grateful for a connection to nature when birdsong washes over you – whether it's from blackbirds roosting in the trees on a city street, or warblers in the hedgerows surrounding farmland.

Here are just a few magical songbirds to start our journey into avian awesomeness – do be encouraged to research more into the birds you love or look up any you don't find here. This is merely an introduction to the magic of birds, and there's plenty more out there for you to find.

Blackbirds

Blackbirds at Twilight
Calling, indignant,
Get out of my space
This is my place
I perch at the edge
The edge of worlds
The edge of all things
Guarding the boundary
I am Druid Dubh
But hear me now
For you are still
For you respect
For you listen and understand
Try to connect;
My angry shout swells
Into song so sweet
And while light remains
Hear my soothing strains
As you walk the winding lanes
To your nest.

Called Lon Dubh in Gaeilge (Irish), the blackbird is one of the most liminal birds I have ever encountered. It sings at dawn and dusk, the miniature master of those magical times of transformation. I have always seen it as the guardian of boundaries; it sings only when things are about to change, to mark the edges of time and space and the moment of the pause before movement. It was no surprise for me to discover, then, that many Celts associated the blackbird with death and rebirth. Rhiannon, sometimes considered a Celtic goddess but certainly an otherworldly being who features heavily in the Welsh Mabinogi, is connected to three mystical birds, possibly blackbirds, who have the power over life and death. They could also sing people into a death-like sleep (Chadd; Taylor, 2016).

The blackbird pops up at various moments in Celtic or Celtic-inspired literature, such as on the shoulder of the mysterious Derg Corra in *Finn and the Man in the Tree* (Meyer, 1904). Here the bird shares a nut with Derg Corra, then after Derg splits his apple with a stag waiting at the foot of the tree, they each drink from a white, bronze vessel filled with water, in which swims a trout. I adore this imagery, of this man who shares all that he has with a creature of the earth, a creature of the sea, and a creature of the sky. This feels very druidic to me, and while I wish we knew more about Derg Corra, I also love the mystery, and that the blackbird so often appears at those times of mystery; that which has no explanation, and brings wonder into our lives.

In Greek mythology, the blackbird would die if it ate the luscious seeds of the pomegranate, a tale that seems to link the bird to Persephone, daughter of Demeter and bringer of spring. Persephone was lured into the underworld and kept there (possibly by trickery, possibly of her own accord) by eating the pomegranate, and thus had to live between two worlds; two states. The blackbird, similarly, is most active between two states; between light and darkness.

The Piper at the Gates of Dawn is normally a reference to Pan, from the chapter of the same name in *The Wind in the Willows* by Kenneth Grahame. Over the years, I have transmuted this title into my own private name for the blackbird. Especially in winter, I can be found nursing a hot mug of tea, on the doorstep of my home, listening to the blackbird herald in the sunrise.

Correspondences

- New beginnings
- Dawn
- Dusk
- Transition periods between seasons e.g. late spring into early summer.
- Moments of mystery: a sudden burst of blackbird song may indicate you are in the presence of something magical, or that something significant is about to occur in your life.
- Astral travel
- Physical travel
- Boundaries, both protective and between worlds.
- Portents of death but also of birth, so be careful with this one!

A blackbird feather is a lucky find indeed, and one placed on your altar at the east will not only symbolise air and the spirits of the sky, but be a catalyst for any sacred mysteries you explore whilst using the altar in this state. You may also find that if you honour any Celtic deities, they may become more prominent in your life, or you may be more aware of them while the feather remains.

Blackbirds are quite prone to leucism, a genetic disorder akin to albinism which causes a lack of pigment in the feathers. I remember a school trip where the teacher pointed out a white blackbird that was hopping around the park. He said that the pale bird had been there every year he had been bringing students. I was fascinated, but it wasn't until much later that I learnt that white variants of normally darker creatures are often messengers from the 'other world'; either beyond the veil, where the dead reside, or from inside the hollow hills where otherworldly beings dwell. Either way, seeing a blackbird with either partial or full white plumage means you are likely being watched by something not of our realm. This is one reason why blackbirds are often connected to death and birth, as these are the points in our lives when we are closest to the hidden realms.

Visualisation and pathworking are great ways to build a relationship with birds, especially if you don't live in the most rural of areas, or can't get outside at the times when the birds are active. Visualisation is the practice of imagining something in your mind – not everyone can do this, so if you struggle with this, audio descriptions or focusing on images can help. Pathworking tends to be a guided journey, often with another person or using a pre-recorded script to help you direct your consciousness to a particular destination. You can try using either of these techniques to connect more strongly to birds. Yes, blackbirds are common enough, even in quite built-up areas, but if you are working ten-hour days in the heart of winter, you may miss those liminal dawn and dusk moments that are the key times to spot these beautiful songbirds.

Seeing a blackbird in visualisations or meditation may mean you are on the cusp of a great change in your life. It may also mean that something that has been static or stagnant in your life for a long time will start to resolve itself, or move forwards. This could be a stale relationship, a job you feel stuck in, or perhaps a period of depression. I suffer from quite low periods of depression, and the blackbirds' song always reminds me that change is coming. It may not be tomorrow, or the day after, but at some point, I will open my eyes and the sun will have risen on my shadowy mind. After all, as the saying goes, it's always darkest before dawn.

Walking with my boy
We listen to the song
That has always tugged at my heartstrings
Since I was as tiny as him.

The evening is just over halfway gone
The sky purplish
As the light wanes
And who do we hear?
Lon Dubh
Messenger of the twilight
Guardian at the gates.
I point him out to my boy
And we watch his chest pump
And his beak bob
As atop the neighbour's roof
He marks his spot in the world
His high point
His territory.
And as the light finally wanes
The blackbird silhouette
Remains on our eyes
For the rest of the walk.

Wrens

The wren represents deceit and trickery, but also skill and a keen eye. The wren hid himself on the eagle's back while the great bird of prey soared higher and higher, then as the eagle tired, the wren launched himself skywards, claiming the title 'King of Birds' (Aesop, referenced by Plutarch, *Praecepta Gerendae Reipublicae* approx. A.D. 96). There is a tale in the *Mabinogion* of the boy who fells a wren with a single fling of a stone. The boy is Llew, son of Arianrhod, who was hidden from her as she refused to name him. His name means 'he of the skilled hand,' a similar epithet to one held by the Irish God King Lugh. Arianrhod accidentally bestowed the name on him, after exclaiming at his skill in hitting the tiny bird with one thrown stone. Young Llew, via his guardian Gwydion, also gains arms and a wife through duplicitous means, however, he would have had no need of deceit had his mother acknowledged him in the first place.

In some First Nations customs, the wren is a bird of war, as it carries within it more courage than is indicated by its tiny size.

Correspondences

- Poetry
- Song
- Deceit/duplicity
- Lies/preparing to lie
- Practical skill
- Honing a craft to perfection
- Winning
- Ambition
- Taking advantage of others
- Defeating a larger foe
- Winter's end
- Hiding/invisibility/hiding one's attributes
- Bravery and courage

- Foolishness
- Protectiveness, especially over one's family
- Fierceness

I'm always astonished by the sheer volume of the wren's voice. If one happens to be in the birch tree when I step into my back garden, the sharp scolding I receive is completely at odds with the bird's tiny size. Even the cats look concerned when the wren starts on them. The wren is a symbol that we are all capable of great things, even that which may seem impossible to others. This reminds us not to let others put us down, or to listen to nay-sayers. If you want to do something, just go do it.

The wren is also fiercely protective over its territory like most birds, but with particularly vocal viciousness! Seeing a wren in meditation may indicate that there is something you are not willing to share, and the context of the visualisation will tell you whether this is a good thing or not. A fleeing wren in a winter's scene may indicate that there is something you are clinging onto which you really should let go of. After all, based on what we know of folklore, the wren is showing you a situation in which it is likely to die. However, a wren shouting from a safe place on a sunny morning may indicate that there is something you should keep to yourself, and that you are perfectly correct in not letting anyone share it with you.

If you have something you really need to go for, a job perhaps, or a new venture, or perhaps an athletic venture such as a marathon or similar, place an image of the wren in a sacred place, such as an altar or near your bed for when you go to sleep. You may find the tiny bird's courage seeping into you, and giving you the motivation you need. If you dream of the wren, record your dreams as soon as you awake, as you may find these dreams fade quickly. The wren is a master of camouflage, and just as it can be hard to spot in the woods or garden, it can be a sneaky visitor in visualisations and dreams.

Wrens are a symbol of the *file*, or the Irish bard; weavers of words for satire and story alike. When you see a wren, you are seeing part of nature's story; a noisy little chapter that really wants you to take note, and listen.

> To them I was not human
> but a stone or tree:
> I felt a sharp wonder
> they could not feel.

Excerpt from *A Necklace of Wrens*, by Michael Hartnett, 1987.

Sharp wonder is a wonderful turn of phrase, and so apt here. The wren is a tiny bird, but with a huge voice and bold personality. It is a tiny, feathery bundle of contradictions, and has been inspiring humans through folklore and superstition for millennia. We are wondrous in the presence of the wren; we don't understand how something so tiny can be so resilient and tough, and throughout history we have tried to figure it out through tales of deceit, betrayal and heroism. As a witch, I see birds as both a physical creature, wondrous and magical in their own right, but also as an incredible source of magical symbolism. By studying the wren's appearance in history and mythology, we can sketch out a useful list of correspondences and symbolism to help us in magical and spiritual practice.

Key Folklore Snippet: King of the Birds

It was possibly Aesop who first told this tale, which is referenced by Plutarch around A.D. 96. In Glen-na-hEan, the valley of the birds, the inhabitants were trying to choose a king. An owl and two swans decided that the only way to decide this was to have a competition; whoever could fly highest would be crowned King of the Birds. Everyone was pretty certain that the eagle had this one in the bag, but as the eagle soared higher than anyone else, he became tired, and confident that he had won, began to relax and drift downwards. At that point, the wren took off from where he had been perched on the eagle's back, flew the highest, and won the title. Although the wren had won unfairly, the birds conceded that a king needs to be clever as well as strong, and so the wren was named King of the Birds.

This is an interesting tale, as it kind of promotes dishonesty and cheating! It would be easy to say that this proves that the wren is associated with lies, deception, and maybe even using others to get what you want. And indeed, at times, the wren absolutely can mean these things, especially when seen in dreams. However, there is another perspective. The eagle in the tale is a bit of a bully; he is sure he will win as he is the biggest and strongest. The wren literally uses the eagle's strength against him, and proves that brains ultimately overcome brawn. In this context, the wren represents wit, intelligence, ambition, and working to your own strengths.

From a magical perspective, a picture of a wren in your sacred space can remind you that although there may be others who are better than you at certain things, if you focus on your own skills and powers, you will ultimately be successful in your goals. If you remain uncertain about a path you are on, suddenly seeing a wren or hearing a wren's call can be a nudge from nature to examine what you are doing, and if it is in tune with your true self; are you doing something because you feel like you should, rather than because it is something you love? The wren is a symbol of anyone being able to achieve anything if they put their mind to it; of drive, motivation, and sheer grit.

In one of my songs, *Dance of Brigid*, I mention the wren being hunted at winter's end. This is a real tradition that continued even in the last century in places including Ireland, Wales, certain parts of England, and the South of France. There are many tales that explain why the wren was hunted. On the Isle of Man, Tehi Tegi was a goddess who lured besotted men to their watery deaths in a river. She escaped justice by turning into a wren, but was banished from the Isle, and when returning annually, was hunted for her crime. A nasty side effect of this tale is that for some time, women were made to walk on foot whilst men were comfortable on horseback, as if all women had to pay for the misdemeanours of one "wanton" goddess.

The 26th of December is Boxing Day for most of Britain, and also St Stephen's Day. In parts of Ireland, it is also known as Wren Day, Wren's Day or even Hunt the Wren Day, a title leaving little to the imagination. In recent years, a fake wren was hunted, but traditionally a real wren would be caught, caged and either killed or kept alive by the whim of the mummers and the crowd that came to watch them.

It's possible that the wren was a symbol of the winter, perhaps because it is not migratory and therefore one of the few songbirds still visible during the colder months. Killing the wren was killing winter; ending the cold and dark and rejoicing in the imminent return of the sun.

As modern pagans, we (hopefully!) recognise that it is not necessary to sacrifice the poor bird in order to bring back spring. We can still utilise the traditional aspects of this part of the wren's history to positive effect though. A wren's feather (a rare find but if they have nested in your garden, you may find some) is a symbol of seasonal transition, particularly the move into spring. It's an ideal addition to any Imbolc display, or to the eastern part of your sacred space. It's a potent symbol of air, new beginnings, and light.

At a deeper level, the wren is a metaphor for letting go of stagnant or damaging aspects of your own life. If there is a transitional period in your own life that you are struggling with, the wren can be a smart little guide to help you through this, and can even point you in the direction of other assistance you may require. I had a wren come and shout at me in the garden, when I was feeling particularly depressed once. It clung to the wall, bobbed its head almost angrily at my slightly scanty herb patch, and then flew off so fast it almost seemed to vanish. I looked at the straggly herbs and realised I had been meaning to improve this section of the garden for a while, and that it had been bothering me more than I realised. I immediately set to work on this, adding new herbs and caring better for the ones I had, and the joy I gained from this helped so much with my mental state.

Be the wren; let your voice be heard and fly high!

Thrushes

Thrushes are members of the *Turdidae* family and many have a scientific name beginning with *Turdus*. They appear all over the world, and make the most beautiful music as they mark their territory and scour it for insects and other treats. In the UK, we have only two birds that we call "thrush": The mistle thrush and the song thrush. However, it may surprise readers to learn that we actually have six thrushes you can spot across Britain and Ireland, including some that only visit these shores seasonally.

The aforementioned blackbird is a type of thrush, although very distinctive thanks to the male's glossy, black plumage and banana-yellow beak. You could even call the blackbird the ultimate thrush, as its scientific name is *Turdus turdus*, literally Latin for "Thrush thrush." So good, they named it twice.

The ring ouzel, *Turdus torquatus*, is a summer visitor, spotted nesting in rocky crags. It's also black but smaller than the blackbird and with a striking white bib that sets it apart from its native cousins.

Fieldfares and redwings come to us in the winter from colder areas like Scandinavia. Resilient little beasts, they can fly hundreds of miles in a single night to reach warmer climes. One Solstice morning, I sat in the kitchen, wondering what the flock of birds was in the distance sycamore tree. Everything else was frosty and quiet, but these birds made the tree quiver, 20-30 of them, weighing down the thinner branches. My husband took a look with his super-zoom camera, and we could just see the blush of orange where the wing meets the body. Beautiful redwings, probably just arrived from Scandinavia, resting after a long, cold night in the chilled winter air. What a beautiful Solstice gift that was.

Moving across the Atlantic to North America, there are many more species of thrush such as the hermit thrush, Swainson's thrush, and Bicknell's thrush. The American robin is also a member of the thrush family and not related to the European robin at all. It's simply named so for its glowing orange breast. It's probably one of the most common thrushes to spot in a garden or yard, particularly if you hang a bird feeder or fill a bird bath. A natural pond or pool is also attractive to them, as they gather mud here with which to help build their nests. One thing they have in common with their European counterparts is their omnivorous diet. If you can add mealworms to your feeder, you might see more robins and other thrushes coming to feed.

There are at least 21 distinct thrush species in North America, many of which migrate to South America as winter approaches. While all have their own significance and folklore, here are some of the general correspondences and associations connected to thrushes.

Correspondences and Associations
My first observation about the thrush is that they just. Keep. Going! They are so resilient and can fly for hundreds of miles in a single journey. They rest, they eat, then they move again. Incredible. If you've ever wanted a bird to represent determination and resilience, you could do worse than choosing a thrush.

Other correspondences include:

- Transformation
- Personal growth
- New beginnings
- Poetry and song
- Nostalgia
- Unrequited love
- Agility
- Tenacity
- Adaptability
- Luck
- Learning new languages

Folklore

In Britain and Ireland, the mistle thrush holds a special place in folklore. Its scientific name, *Turdus viscivorus*, translates to "mistletoe-devouring thrush." The common name follows directly on from this and, yes, this bird does love mistletoe berries. Does that connect it to Druidry, and other paths where mistletoe is sacred? That's a possibility, although this association would be entirely modern.

The mistle thrush has an incredibly distinctive call, trilling, high, and powerful. After all, it is the largest thrush *and* songbird in the UK – although as we've seen from the tales of the wren's cry, size isn't everything!

Thrushes are still present in winter – more so, in a way, because of all the additional visitations we have from migrant thrushes like redwings. However, the song thrush is more or less silent until spring. So, hearing the thrush's song for the first time in a year is a clear message that the new season is on the way.

Other common names for the mistle thrush include Big Mavis, Jeremy Joy, and Mizzly Dick. Hearing a thrush may indicate that a storm is on the way, or other inclement weather.

There used to be an English folk belief that mistletoe would only grow once it had passed through the digestive system of a thrush. However, it's far more likely that the birds spread the plant by cleaning their sticky beaks on the bark of trees, inadvertently "planting" seeds from the berries here.

Magic

Meditate on the mistle thrush to find your way to a new beginning.

If you find a thrush feather, place it on your altar or in your sacred space, or in a pouch upon your person, to bring luck in material matters such as career or wealth.

Thrushes use whatever they can find to make nests, from litter to threads to mud. Consider your own nest: Are you a thrush, re-using and upcycling effectively, or a magpie, hoarding shiny items that are less practical? Decide which you prefer and work towards a more balanced living space, if necessary.

If you're having family troubles, particularly regarding children, you can channel the energy of the thrush. They are fierce parents, often fighting off opportunistic scavengers and predators in order to protect their eggs and chicks.

Robins

The robin comes every day now
Brown and red
Earth and fire
Creature of air
Sitting serenely on the wicker pot
Hopping from fence to tree
Looking through the window
Head cocked in curiosity
I think we all mimic
Without realising
Three humans standing
Rapt
Motionless
With heads to one side
While the robin assesses us
Calm
Confident
Free
And nabs the rice crispies
I threw out this morning.

The European robin, *Erithacus rubecula*, is perhaps one of the most familiar UK winter birds, thanks to any number of greetings cards showing snowy scenes with these red-breasted birds up front and centre. Robins are actually present in the UK all year round, but perhaps more noticeable in winter as other species migrate away – plus we get a few additional robin visitors coming over from the continent. Robins are brave and will often come very close to humans, especially if you've been turning the earth in the garden or allotment and there's the chance of a juicy worm!

Correspondences

- Bravery
- Viciousness (robins will fight to the death for their territory!)
- Beauty in simplicity
- Fire
- Blood
- Kindness
- Generosity
- Otherworldly messages

Folklore

An 1868 edition of *Note and Queries* records a belief that if one should let a robin die in their hands, their hands will shake forevermore. In general, there are a number of beliefs that state that it is very bad luck to harm or kill a robin.

There is a Christian tale that the robin got his red breast from fanning the flames of a fire to keep the baby Jesus warm (Egan, 1988). In another, the red is from the blood of Jesus Christ on his way to the crucifixion.

Both male and female robins have the lovely, glowing, reddish-orange breast feathers, so there is a lovely symbol of equality with the robin.

It's considered bad luck to tamper with a robin's nest or steal their eggs.

Magic

If you ever need courage to face a difficult situation, look to the robin. They will defend their territory and their food sources to the death. They are fierce, incredibly protective, and can be aggressive. Channel this aggression into assertiveness to move through your situation as you see fit. Wear red or orange to remind yourself of the robin, or listen to a recording of the robin's song as you fall asleep. If you dream of robins, it could be a sign that you are much stronger than you think you are.

Some sources state that the robin is sacred to Thor, and that harming a robin or its nest would cause the perpetrator to be struck by lightning (Tate, 2007). If you follow this reasoning, then using an image of a robin or a fallen robin feather on a Thor altar or sacred space could be a good move.

There is a legend of a robin who gave monks an ear of corn that fed them and their community many times over (Tate, 2007). You could call on the robin in a time of need or hunger, whether literal or spiritual.

Orioles

How wonderful to get the opportunity to learn about and then write about a type of bird (or, really, several types of birds) that I've only seen in books, films, and TV shows. Oh, and as the inspiration for some Pokémon! Orioles include several birds in the *Icteridae* family, a group of 108 species collectively called *New World Blackbirds*. The scientific name comes from the Ancient Greek term for jaundice and refers to the bright yellow plumage many of this family have.

Orioles account for about 32 members of this family, and they all have, without exception, a mixture of black and yellow or orange feathers – the dullest shade is a rich, chestnut brown. Some are almost totally black, like the epaulet oriole of South America, however, even this species has a splash of yellow on its wing.

There are also Old World orioles, that occupy large areas of Asia, Australasia, and Africa. However, they are entirely unrelated to their American counterparts.

Arguably the most famous American oriole is the Baltimore oriole, resplendent in ochre with a black-brown head and dark and white banding on its wings. This oriole has both a trilling song and several piping calls, often heard when it's high up in a tree. They can also screech when defending their nests.

Correspondences and Associations

- Survival against the odds; fighting adversity
- Opportunism
- Humility
- Industriousness
- Partnership with nature
- One good turn deserves another

Folklore

The Hopi peoples of North America believe that orioles are guardians of the direction of North.

The Pima associate orioles with the sun, perhaps due to their gaudy plumage. They have special songs and dances for the oriole.

In the tale of the oriole and the pecan tree, the pecan tree shelters the oriole and his family from a terrible storm. To return the favour, the oriole discovers that a false spring has caused the trees to bud too early, and manages to warn the pecan tree that a cold snap is on the way. The pecan doesn't put its buds out, and manages to avoid the freezing north wind that would have chilled its new, fragile buds. Today, the orchard oriole is still found in pecan trees, showing the strength of the partnership the two beings made.

Magic

Finding an oriole feather can mean a storm is on the way, either literal or not – it could be that something in your life is about to turn tumultuous. The oriole is providing you a warning and time to prepare yourself, or to look out for other warnings.

If you need to be more discerning in life or in a particular situation, consider channelling the energy of the oriole. This picky eater won't just go for anything. It takes its time to source the food it prefers, and will bypass other nutritious food in favour of its favourites. The oriole is a reminder that it's okay not to settle, and sometimes waiting and searching is the answer rather than grabbing the first thing that comes along.

You can attract orioles by growing or setting out dark berries such as cherries and dark-coloured grapes – most orioles will ignore green/white grapes and other pale fruits.

Warblers

The term "warbler" is used for a number of small perching birds, and doesn't necessarily group them by species or family. In fact, there are at least two distinct "superfamilies" of warblers; one that's mostly found in the Americas (Passeroid warblers) and one immense family with hundreds of species all over the rest of the world (Sylviid warblers).

New World Warblers is a collection of around 120 species, thought to have originated in Central America. These birds are, like the orioles, striking in colour and song, from the sharp, tilting tweets of the prothonotary warbler (*Protonotaria citrea*) to the up-and-down "Teacher, Teacher!" call of the ovenbird (*Seiurus aurocapilla*).

In the UK, warblers are less brightly coloured, tending toward easily camouflaged greens and browns. Birdwatchers often note how fast and agile they are, flitting from branch to branch sometimes faster than the eye can see. The most easily spotted is probably the blackcap, *Sylvia atricapilla*, a small, grey-brown bird with a distinctive dark patch on its head that sets it apart from other warblers. In contrast, there's Cetti's warbler, with just over 3,000 male birds accounted for across our islands. It's rare and also hard to spot thanks to its brown plumage – a rarity that most birdwatchers would be delighted to add to their record.

Correspondences and Associations

- Camouflage, hiding in plain sight
- Saying what needs to be said
- Good things come in small packages
- Unexpected beauty
- Song and music
- Perseverance
- Change
- Joy

Folklore

In some parts of England, the blackcap is known as the Northern Nightingale or Mock Nightingale because its high, flute-like song is so beautiful.

Magic

If you hear a warbler while out in the woods, take a moment to listen to the song and make a note of how it makes you feel. Focus on your connection to the place you're in, the bird itself, and how that also connects you to the past. After all, warblers have been making this world musical for thousands of years.

Think about what you would say if you had no filter and nothing holding you back – you don't have to say it, but let the warbler guide you to a realisation of what you want and the direction you need your life to go in.

As we come to the end of this chapter on songbirds, I am moved to think about the way birds communicate – with each other and with us. I was watching two gulls recently, while staying with family on the East Coast of Yorkshire. They did their loud, wailing cry, but then once one had flown towards the other, they started a different conversation. They chuckled and made noises more akin to a dog barking. One pointed out some food that had been left on some steps, and made a strange chuffing sound. The other replied with a strangled warble and hopped down.

It turns out that herring gulls have an amazing range of vocalisations. It's easy to write them off as cawing, shrieking nuisances. But when you've spent a decent amount of time at the coast listening to them, especially when they're just sat "talking" to each other, you start to hear tone, phrasing, and what's all too easy to anthropomorphise as humour. A sound suspiciously like a crying baby, a high-pitched squeal, and a chuffing laugh all fall way outside the typical soaring cries heard on every backing track for a seaside TV show. They're fascinating and alarming - so human sounding at times, yet so utterly removed from us. When combined with the neighbouring Jackdaws' human-sounding chatter, the impression of two slightly antagonistic families having a chelp at each other is hard to ignore.

There's a whole language happening right in front of us and we may never speak it, but my word, does it speak to us.

The way different bird sounds evoke different emotions and memories; those gulls give me the sweet nostalgia of the seaside; blackbirds, the fizzy energy of twilight; an owl, the haunting loneliness of the deep night.

Songbirds are truly magnificent, but bird-magic seekers, look to all the music of the birds for a complete soundscape of nature.

Chapter 2

Carrion Eaters

It's not easy, being green
She laughs, and tosses hair of flame
Whilst directing me to clean up
Alder trees
Wasteland
Abandoned buddleia
Whilst nudging me up the hillside
Starting compost piles
Feeding the birds
And not just the "pretty" ones
As I place bacon fat
On the grass
And duck inside away
From probing beaks
Of magpies, crows
Jackdaws now the spring has
Yes, sprung
And today, a kite
A red kite
Tail forked in flight
But straight and serene
Sitting on my fence
A bird once considered
Nothing but a pest
Then a rubbish cleaner
Scavenger extraordinaire
Now a valued member
Of our ecosystem
We learn, we understand

She sits, she eats, she leaves
My garden is clean, her babies are fed
I nod to the sky
To the land
To the liminal spaces between
To Her
And while I wonder
About honour and worship
A pair of robins
Start a home
Oblivious.

Scavengers are nature's cleaners. We might feel our gorge rising when we watch a crow ripping a dead pigeon to shreds (a sight I have seen every time I've visited London, without exception!), but without them, who will clean that up? The corpse would fester and rot, and attract dangerous volumes of insects and bacteria. The scavengers, the carrion eaters, are the clean-up crew we all need, and scavenging birds are particularly fascinating, often with complex social structures and high levels of intelligence.

Magpies

Pica pica, the delightful Latin name for a Magpie, on its lonesome is a portent of doom, but a group of magpies is a mischief, a word which seems so much lighter and cheekier. But for a long time, it was presumed that magpies were actually really bad news for other birds.

Magpies will eat baby birds and eggs during the breeding season, when their own babies are hungry and there aren't enough insects, carrion, or fruit to feed both parents and chicks. This has given them a bad reputation as baby killers, and it was thought for many years that magpies were having a detrimental effect on the population of songbirds such as blackbirds and thrushes.

However, studies have proven that even when the magpie population increases by as much as 5%, songbird populations do not show any significant decline: good news for bird lovers everywhere (RSPB, 2021). The prime predator of our beloved songbirds is actually the domestic cat, not the poor, much-maligned magpie. Plus, songbirds are also in decline due to loss of habitat and other human-caused environmental factors. It's a bit rich of us to blame to magpies.

Magpies are also great parents and fiercely protective of their own chicks.

Correspondences and Associations

- Wealth and prosperity
- Vanity
- Pride
- Hidden beauty
- Intelligence
- Family
- Protection

Folklore

One for Sorrow
Two for Joy
Three for a Girl
Four for a Boy
Five for Silver
Six for Gold
Seven for a Secret
Ne'er to be told.

Remember this rhyme? I touched on it in the introduction, but here is the full version I learnt growing up. Most of us will know some version of that rhyme, a strange form of avian divination that relies upon there never being eight magpies or more. But have you also heard:

Once a Wish
Twice a Kiss
Thrice a Letter
Four, something better...

I was taught this as a little girl, but it was also interchangeable as a sneezing rhyme. It was a shame the sneezes always seemed to stop at three, meaning we never found out what the 'something better' was. The wonderful Terry Pratchett also gave this alternative version in the Discworld novel, *Carpe Jugulum*:

One for Sorrow
Two for Mirth
Three for a Funeral
Four for a Birth
Five for Heaven
Six for Hell
Seven's the De'il
His ane Sel.

I think his point was how interchangeable superstitions are, and how easily they become transformed between locales and the ages, whilst still retaining the similar sense of foreboding.

Another well-known magpie superstition is to salute the birds if you should happen to see them. Or to say 'Hello' and touch your forelock. I always say, "Good day," to the magpies, but then again, I say, "Hello," to most birds!

All these superstitions (except the sneeze rhyme) revolve around the idea that to see a lone magpie is bad luck, and by acknowledging the bird you are breaking the curse; dispelling the bad vibes, so to speak. The bird holds no power over you if you note its appearance and speak of it out loud. It's also a way of showing respect to the birds; if they believe you respect them, perhaps they will not pass on their bad luck to you. Some say good morning to the magpie and wish its partner well, thus reinforcing the idea that somewhere, another magpie is lurking, thus bringing good luck instead of bad.

One local superstition holds that to see a crow immediately after a magpie cancels any bad luck, which just shows how much we revere corvids in this part of the world, and how much power we associate with them.

Magic

From a source of divination via a superstitious rhyme to a cure for epilepsy, magpies have long been associated with magic and witchcraft. If you are interested in including a little bird magic in your everyday practice or meditation, here are a few correspondences and associations that can help bring the magic of the magpie into your life.

Wealth: Magpies have a notorious reputation for being attracted to shiny objects, as do many other corvids. The idea that magpies are thieves actually comes from a nineteenth-century French play, although magpies are naturally inquisitive. This idea of the magpie yearning for trinkets is so deeply rooted in our collective subconsciousness that it's still a powerful tool for magic or visualisation. Meditating on the magpie or including foraged feathers on your altar or in your ritual space can be useful in magic to attract wealth or prosperity. Be aware of the temptation towards greed and obsession though, as these are also aspects of the magpie. Careful accumulation of necessary wealth is not the same as avarice.

Hidden Beauty and Mystery: It's easy to assume the magpie is simply black and white, but take a good look as it hops around on a sunny day, and you will see a rainbow of blues and greens suddenly blaze from those black feathers. The iridescence of the magpie reminds us to look for hidden magic in everyday life, and that beauty isn't just about what we see at first glance. The magpie is a reminder to look beyond the surface and to be grateful for fleeting moments of inspiration.

Pride and Vanity: The magpie struts around as if it owns the place, lording it over your garden or the woods, even the streets of your local town. It can be an incredible totem of pride; of keeping your head held high in difficult situations, or of putting yourself forward and being proud of your achievements. This can be useful when developing magic or spells to help you get a new job, start a new creative venture, or for simply gaining a confidence boost if you are going through a period of self-doubt or when your self-esteem has taken a knock. However, the magpie is also associated with vanity, so be aware of the temptation to preen and lose yourself in overblown self-importance.

Intelligence: The magpie, like most corvids, is extremely intelligent. They are in the same intelligence bracket as many of the great apes, and have been known to demonstrate highly developed social rituals, including the ability to show grief. The magpie is particularly associated with communication and the ability to get an important message across. In dreams, the appearance of a magpie may indicate a dissatisfaction with a current situation or relationship, and that this may be resolved by speaking openly and listening to what the other person has to say.

I see the magpie as the orca of the sky. Iridescently black and white, glossy and beautiful, dangerous to some but so mesmerising to watch. They are large, strong, and surprisingly brave. Many times, I have seen a lone magpie successfully see off a hungry cat; an amazing sight indeed, and a very puzzling and frustrating experience for the cat! Keep an eye out for the magpies in your local area, listen out for their unusual, almost voice-like cries, and remember to give a nod to one of the most recognisable birds in British folklore.

There's a pair of magpies that seem to guard my garden. In fact, there's a whole family of them, but the adults remain close and train their babies, then the young ones move on while the adults stay here. One of the youths was particularly cocky last year, and saw off a huge ginger and white tom cat that was trying to mark its territory, which would have annoyed our cat no end. They're good guardians, and I'm happy that they come to visit us.

Ravens

In some of the corvid groups I'm in on social media, there's a general guide to checking if you've seen a raven. If you *think* you've seen a raven, it's probably a large crow. If you think, "Oh my goodness, what is that enormous bird, it's so big, how can it be that big?!" then it's most likely a raven.

Of course, there are other distinctions – a wider beak and a diamond-shaped tail in flight, for example – but the raven is surely one of the most impressive birds, size-wise, that we have in the UK. They can grow over two feet in length and can have a wingspan of up to five feet. Imagine, a local bird with a wingspan wider than some adults' height!

Common ravens, *Corvus corax*, are members of the crow family. They're quite long-lived, with a lifespan of up to 17-18 years in the wild and over 40 years in captivity. Ravens are also notoriously intelligent, able to mimic human speech and solve complex problems.

I had an experience with an intelligent raven. I was at an animal rescue centre in the far north of England, many years ago. There was a huge raven in a massive aviary, perched near the bars at the front. I wandered over and said, "Hello," and the raven "Kronked" at me in return. She tipped her head to one side and blinked at me. I was holding a cup of duck food in one hand, and I stepped closer to listen to the raven. She started making quiet, chuffing vocalisations. So, I stepped right up to the bars to hear better. Quick as a flash, she grabbed the edge of the cup and simply tipped it down so that the food all spilled onto the floor. With a final "Kronk!" of triumph, she hopped down and started enjoying her prize.

Many other birds and animals would have tried to get in the cup, pecking toward the food itself. She knew, within seconds, that tipping the cup would give her the greatest prize. Remarkable animals.

Correspondences and Associations

- Magic, sorcery
- Divination
- Protection, particularly guarding others or guarding buildings and structures
- Death, decay
- Transformation
- Survival
- Mischief
- Chaos
- Thought and understanding
- Memory

Ravens are also associated with specific deities including the Greek God Apollo, the Norse God Odin, and some postulate that the Irish Goddess An Mórrígan is connected to ravens, although the more common association is crows. However, some tales merely refer to her transforming into a "black bird," so this is open to interpretation. Badb, often seen as a sister of An Mórrígan and/or an aspect of the same, is most strongly associated with black corvids.

Folklore

Several Pacific Northwest indigenous peoples revere the raven as the creator of the world. However, others consider the raven a trickster being. These can be two separate beings or possibly two aspects of the same being. In some tales, it is the raven's trickery that causes the world to come into being. The raven may have stolen the sun, and tempted humanity to come from within a seashell into the world.

Some indigenous Russian peoples, for example, the Chuckchi of Siberia, tell tales of a raven spirit called Kutkh. Kutkh let light into the world by pecking at the stones keeping it out. A sneeze caused by mice in Kutkh's nasal passages caused the mountains to be created. When Kutkh tried to stamp the mountains back into place, the great bird inadvertently created the oceans.

The Norse God Odin's ravens are called Huginn, which means *thought* and Muninn, which means *Memory*. These great birds often perch on Odin's shoulders. He taught them to speak, and they often travel the world, discovering what's going on and reporting this information back to the God. Sometimes, Odin is referred to as Hrafnaguð, which simply means "Raven God."

The raven is a prominent bird in Welsh folklore, with both Brân and Branwen, important figures in the *Mabinogi*, named for the bird.

Magic

Hearing a raven's call can be a portent, not necessarily of doom, but certainly of change or transformation. If there is a period of change coming in your life, ensure you're ready for any eventuality and don't stint on preparation time.

Seeing a raven feed might mean something unpleasant is about to be removed from your life. This could be anything from stress to a job you hate to a physical object.

If you see a raven in a visualisation or dream, it could be a sign that you'll be receiving some important information soon. Make a note of any other symbols present to understand this message more clearly.

Jackdaws

Hey
Miss it once
Hey
Look up
Two jackdaws in a sycamore tree

One edged along the main branch
Blinking down at me in curiosity
Sharing the autumn sun
All three cloaked against the autumn wind
The two birds aren't hunting
Or foraging
Simply resting and being;
At the most, marking their territory:
Enjoying their existence
Reminding me not to feel guilty
About doing the same.

Corvus monedula, first described formally by the 18th-century zoologist Carl Linnaeus, is known commonly as the jackdaw; a hooded thief who can steal hearts as easily as it steals trinkets. Like all corvids, this bird holds a special place in human myth and folklore, although is often overlooked in favour of its larger cousins, the crow and the raven.

Jackdaws are one of the few animals other than humans to use their eyes to communicate, and study the eyes of other animals in order to ascertain their intent (Auguste von Bayern, University of Oxford). The jackdaw has beautiful, silvery, almost other-worldly eyes that seem incredibly perceptive, even more so than animals we generally consider intelligent such as dogs and other primates. Jackdaws watch where the eyes focus, rather than where the head turns, and do the same not just amongst their own kind but as they observe other animals too. This allows them to be master thieves, snatching food out literally from under the noses of slower creatures as soon as the victim has even spotted the tasty morsel. They represent observation, brain over brawn and above all, downright cheek!

Jackdaws are relatively small; the second smallest corvid, ahead only of the colourful and noisy jay. Like many small but successful animals, they show us that size isn't everything.

If you are feeling inadequate, lacking in strength, or swept uncontrollably by a tide of events, take a lesson from the jackdaw. It is small, but it perseveres. It looks to its family and friends for help. It communicates, often loudly, and does not stand alone. These are all helpful reminders that we are not islands, and reaching out for assistance can sometimes be the best course of action. Remember to speak up for what you believe in, and when your voice is not heard, join your voice with that of others who share your beliefs. Strength in numbers is the jackdaw motto!

Correspondences and Associations

- Weather divination
- Wealth
- Pride
- Vanity
- Prophecy
- Conflict
- Conversation
- Family
- Home
- Socialisation
- Freedom
- Opportunism

Folklore

In Ireland, jackdaws were once kept as pets. However, their penchant for stealing shiny trinkets led to someone who was a hoarder or thief being called "As bad as jackdaws." (Mac Coitir, 2015).

A jackdaw on the roof may indicate a new arrival is on the way. Such folk superstitions are common and change from area to area, however, it's worth noting that the year the jackdaws moved into our roof in force, was the year I found out I was having an unexpected baby, just before the Winter Solstice.

Magic

Rain: Ovid wrote that the jackdaw was a harbinger of rain. Call upon the spirit of the jackdaw in your meditations or pathworking and visualise the weather changing. Move yourself into a calming downpour, or imagine a light summer rain refreshing you as you walk your path. See if you can use this to influence the weather, perhaps as a gardening aid!

Money: Jackdaws are notorious in mythologies as diverse as Christian and Ancient Greek for being unable to resist shiny objects, often gold. If you want to draw money into your life, visualise jackdaws finding precious trinkets and bringing them to you. Don't visualise them stealing belongings from others; this kind of magic may bite you in the unmentionables if someone decides to retaliate!

Vanity: The jackdaw is supposedly infatuated with its own reflection. If you want the spirit of the jackdaw to visit you in meditation or dreams, leave a bowl of oil out in your sacred space, to lure the bird to come and admire itself. Make sure the bowl is shallow; in the Greek myth, the bird fell in the bowl and was captured. You only want the jackdaw to visit, not to be trapped and possibly angry!

Prophecy: All corvids seem to be associated with prophecy; crows, raven and rooks as well as the cheeky little jackdaw. The jackdaw is particularly drawn to endings and beginnings; a liminal bird that exists on the edge of mortal boundaries such as life and death.

Conflict: Czech folklore holds that quarrelling jackdaws forewarn of an oncoming war. Jackdaws naturally squabble; it's part of how they establish hierarchy in their social structures. If you witness this boisterous behaviour, beware of forthcoming conflict in your own life. This may be a time to hold your tongue, listen before speaking and to be especially mindful of the emotions and moods of those around you.

Talkativeness: Gregory the Theologian wrote that 'The swans will sing when the jackdaws are silent', meaning that wise words come once mindless chatter has stopped. The seemingly ceaseless cries of the jackdaw may seem like chattering nonsense, but in fact they are anything but mindless. The birds are in constant and vital communication, making their tribe aware of their location, position and status. Jackdaws remind us that it's good to talk, and a jackdaw feather in your sacred space or held during meditation may allow you to find your voice when you are feeling repressed or shy. If you can't find a jackdaw feather, the image of a jackdaw (either photo or painting/drawing) is sufficient.

Freedom: The jackdaw cannot bear to be confined, and will become incredibly depressed if caged. It is the part of our own spirit which longs to be free; which yearns to step outside and run for the hills. Dreams of jackdaws in flight may indicate that there is something you are yearning to do which is being repressed, either by yourself or something else in your life. Hearing the cry of a jackdaw but not being able to see the bird is a sign that there is something just out of reach within your life, and you need to take a step towards what you truly want.

Opportunism: Jackdaws have some odd habits you don't often see in other birds, such as riding around on the backs of sheep. The reason they do this is to steal the ticks that hide in the thick wool (which is obviously good for the sheep too!) and even to steal the wool itself, for their nests. The jackdaw is ingenious, witty and can take advantage of any situation.

This morning, I picked up a jackdaw feather, just outside my front door. I stroked the smooth, black satin and glanced up at the roof, to see if I could see the giver of my gift. I couldn't spy the birds, but I could certainly hear them; that call that's almost akin to a baby's cry emanating from somewhere in the eaves. You see, we're lucky enough to have a whole family of jackdaws living in and around our roof this year, and although they're not the quietest of lodgers, they surely are beautiful.

I placed the feather, quill down, into the soil of a hanging basket and quickly offered up the short prayer: Love, Hope, Family. These are three things I associated with jackdaws, and by focusing on the feather and the original owner, I use these associations to build a safer home for my tribe. The jackdaw's association with family comes from the intensely complex social structures they have amongst their own kind, intricate with hierarchy, trust and communication.

Watch out for jackdaws in rocky and high places, and listen out for their human-like calls. They are closer to us in so many ways than we might like to admit, and help us to take ourselves a little bit less seriously; a vital skill in today's world!

Crows

Crows, black shadows flying overhead; omens of death and war. Feeding on battlefields, their cries signal dark times ahead and earn of evil prophecies. Or do they? Even though the crow is often seen as a harbinger of dark tidings, there is much more to the mythology and folklore of this amazing, intelligent bird than black luck.

Correspondences and Associations
Through the telling of various tales and myths and our own observations we can tie the following correspondences and attributes to the crow:

- Badb
- An Mórrígan
- Nemain (sometimes conflated with Badb)
- Battlefields, the start or end of battle, the aftermath, the oncoming storm
- Wit
- Intellect
- Communication
- Death
- Change
- Moving between worlds
- Mischief
- Devotion (crows mate for life)

Folklore
In *The Wooing of Emer*, a tale from the Ulster Cycle of Irish mythology, we are told that Badb is the same as the Morrigu (The Mórrígan) and that she is the battle crow and a goddess of battle. The word Badb, or Badhbh (pronounced something akin to Bayve) actually means crow, and Badb the goddess is also named Badb Catha, the battle crow. The similarities between the goddess(es) and the bird include the dark shadows they throw over the battlefield, the wailing cries and the stubborn and wilful nature they both seem to have.

Being associated with battle seems to naturally tie in associations with death, which makes sense as the crow is a scavenger; a carrion eater, and a battlefield for a crow is basically an all-you-can-eat buffet with extra juicy bits.

Bresal, King of the Fomorians, named his druid 'Crow', for being wry, witty with words and greedy (source: *The Metrical Dindshenchas*). I used to live with a rescue crow, and I never saw him to be particularly greedy, but he was savvy. If he was full up from eating, sometimes he would take the piece of food I was proffering and hide it away somewhere. Later, I would see him sidle back to his stash and, spying suspiciously around to make sure he was not spotted, he would surreptitiously slide his treasure out for a sneaky snack. Crows can learn to speak, but even without this talent they are fantastic communicators. They can learn to use tools, and even teach other crows about human faces they can trust and those that they can't.

Of course, the crow is important in more than just Celtic folklore and mythology. One of my favourite tales of the crow is the story of the Rainbow Crow. I was lucky enough to see a storyteller perform this live one Yuletide, complete with huge papier-mâché figures and decorations.

This tale is from the Lenin Lenape Tribe of Native Americans. The world was new and had never seen snow. When the snow first fell, the animals thought it was fun. They played and delighted in the soft, wet, cold flakes. But the snow didn't stop. And the animals started to freeze. Worried that they were all going to die, the Wise Owl decided that someone should go as a messenger to Kijiamuh Ka'ong, the Creator Who Creates By Thinking What Will Be. They wanted to petition the creator to bring back the warmth.

The Owl had poor day vision so it was not safe to go. They considered Coyote, but Coyote was easily distracted. They considered Turtle, so safe and reliable, but by the time he returned they would all have frozen. Finally, this important task fell to Rainbow Crow. He was a bird with shimmering feathers all the colours of the rainbow, with a song as beautiful to match.

Rainbow Crow endured an arduous three-day journey without rest, beyond the moon, sun and stars. When he reached the Heavens, he was unsure how to speak to the creator, so he began to sing his most enchanting song.

The Creator was drawn by the song, and wanted to give Rainbow Crow a gift in exchange for the beautiful music. Rainbow Crow begged the Creator to unthink the snow, that the animals might be warm again and not freeze to death. The Creator explained that even the snow and cold have spirits of their own, and cannot be unthought. However, he said he would think of a new thing: fire.

The Creator pushed a stick into the sun, and brought it back, burning bright. He explained that this was fire, and would warm the animals in time of cold. But Rainbow Crow had to hurry back so that the fire didn't burn out before reaching the animals on Earth.

He flew quickly back past the stars, nice and warm from the flames. But then the fire grew closer to his feathers, and as he neared the sun, his tail caught fire. Soon, the flames spread, and by the time he passed the moon, he was black with soot. As he neared Earth, swooping down into the sky, the smoke choked him and he could no longer sing his beautiful song.

So, Rainbow Crow delivered Tindeh, or Fire, to the cold and miserable animals, and all was well and the animals rejoiced. But Rainbow Crow was sad because his beautiful, colourful feathers were gone forever, and the only noise he could make was a raucous caw.

With a breath of wind, the Creator began to speak to Rainbow Crow. He explained that he and all the animals understood the great sacrifice Rainbow Crow had made. In return, the Creator had made it so that the Crow's flesh tasted of smoke, so that nothing and nobody would hunt him. And when people came, they would not put him in a cage to sing, because of his hoarse, cawing voice. He had given the Crow the gift of freedom. But there was one last gift.

The Creator pointed to the Crow's feathers. As the Crow looked on, he saw the blackness dissipate and the hues of the rainbow reappear within each black feather. Sometimes, when the light hits a crowd feather just right, you can still see a touch of colour. And that is a reminder of the great sacrifice that Rainbow Crow made for the whole planet and everyone and everything on it.

Magic

If you are meditating and the image of a crow appears, perhaps the above correspondences may help you decide what the meaning of that is. The same for omens; perhaps a crow flies into your path, or watches you from a nearby building. If you are creating a spell pouch to give you confidence in an interview, perhaps the small image of a crow in the pouch could boost your faith in your communication skills and give you the "gift of the gab".

A Bird Magic Experience: The Crows with the White Feathers

A note on crow magic from several years ago.

We see them every day now. I don't know when they moved in; or maybe they've always been around and we just never noticed them until recently. Three huge, adult crows who always hang around together, hopping along the grass verges outside the local council building.

I saw a meme recently that said 'If you've seen two crows, it's Odin; if there's three crows, it's the Morrigan. Any more crows, and someone's dropped a sandwich!' A fairly accurate summation of our scavenger corvid cousins; they gather where there's food but generally form small, tight social groups.

Crows are not like rooks, with their huge, sprawling rookeries. They are also not like jackdaws, with their intensely convoluted social hierarchies. Locally (to me), even where crows have formed larger groups, you tend to only see two or three out in the open, acting as sentries for the rest of the group. In suburban Yorkshire, it's quite common to see just two or three living together, with no others to look after, presumably as the fledglings have left to form their own 'murders' elsewhere. Crow behaviour varies from group to group; much like humans, they can't be pigeonholed, if you'll excuse the turn of phrase!

The most interesting thing about these particular crow neighbours that I've recently noticed is that they all have white feathers. Not entirely, just a trim of white around the wings. Over the years I have seen many black birds with the odd white feather, but this is the first time I have ever seen three birds of the same species, all with the white feathers on the same part of their body. The dash of white is most noticeable when they're hopping along, with their wings spread slightly to balance their almost comical bobbing about. It's as if they have all dragged their wing tips through a pool of spilled paint; the splashes of white seem random, giving each of the three birds their own individual, quirky look.

White animals have appeared throughout folklore and mythology, not just in my beloved Celtic stories, but across many cultures and traditions. The Lakota people believe that the birth of a white buffalo may herald a period of purification for Mother Earth and the reunification of humanity. A white tiger appears as Bái Hǔ in China and Byakko in Japan, and is a key part of astrology. Returning back to the British Isles, there are tales of white horses, dogs, deer, hare and many more. To generalise, in Celtic mythology the colour white indicates some connection to the underworld, death, or in Irish tales, the aos sí; the people of the hills; fairies, if you will. The overriding theme across all cultures is that a white animal appears at a time of change, transition or transformation; yes, all words with similar meanings, but this transformation can be external or internal; within your control or completely beyond your comprehension.

So why have my friendly, neighbourhood, partially albino (possibly leucistic, a condition that causes pigment in the feathers to be absent) suddenly arrived? Why did I never notice them until the last month, despite having lived here for a year and a half? Well, this year has definitely been a year of changes, and not all good; but not all bad either. There's been illness and trauma among family and friends. We lost a few good people earlier in the year. Some close friends too, suddenly and without warning. On the other side of the wheel, we were, equally unexpectedly, blessed with the news that I was pregnant! There then followed a very difficult pregnancy, with shadows of suspected pre-eclampsia, and very real depression, and a pelvic condition which ended up with me on crutches. The little one was born three weeks ago, and despite the usual new parent fog of fatigue, my health is improving daily, both physically and mentally, and I gradually feel like I'm getting back in touch with the person I remember being.

So, are the crows a symbol of the changes that this year has brought? And are the white feathers a reminder that we are never too far away from the other-worldly, and to remember to acknowledge and respect that? It's definitely given me a lot to think about. A good friend said it was unlikely these birds, so closely associated with the Morrigan and her sister goddesses, would have appeared so suddenly if there wasn't a good reason. A message, perhaps. All I know for sure is we seem to have three unique birds that have made themselves quite at home in our neighbourhood, and I look forward to seeing them each morning now. And the fact that they have made me reflect on the past year and count my blessings is a powerful magic in itself.

Vultures

Vultures are large scavengers found in Europe and both North and South America, as well as Africa and Asia but not Australasia, although evidence suggests they may have existed there long ago. There are 23 species of vulture and they're split into two main groups: Old World vultures and New World vultures. This latter group also includes condors. Despite both groups having many similarities, they're not very closely related at all and are a prime example of convergent evolution; where two species evolve in similar ways despite being largely unrelated.

The collective noun for vulture is flight is called a kettle. Why? I have no idea. A group of roosting vultures is called a committee, while feeding vultures are called a wake – no mystery here. When vultures feed, it means something has died, although not necessarily at their claw. Vultures are patient beasts, often waiting until a corpse is unattended by larger predators before circling gently down to claim the gruesome parts only scavengers long for. For decades, the media has used vultures as a symbol of incoming death. We all know that when the vultures start circling, any struggling hero is in big trouble. However, it may surprise you to learn that the vulture has some fairly contradictory folkloric and mythological associations, and isn't always linked to death and decay.

Correspondences and Associations

In some cultures, vultures are associated with purity. Buddhist sky burials or celestial burials are one example of this. Instead of being buried or burned, the body is left in a high place, ready for scavengers like vultures to pick it clean. In this way, the body is purified, and the vultures are even seen as angels, helping the body make its transference to a new type of existence (Andreoni, 2016). Other correspondences include:

- Resilience – they can eat rotten meat without getting sick thanks to incredibly acidic gastric fluids
- Transformation
- Death but also rebirth
- Connection to the celestial realm
- Maternal instincts
- Social skills, protecting one's friends or community
- The letter or sound *Aleph* in Ancient Egyptian hieroglyphs (the Egyptian vulture)
- The term "Mother" in Ancient Egyptian hieroglyphs (the vulture)
- Cleanliness – eating that which otherwise could cause us and other animals harm
- Asexuality – The Greeks believed that vultures reproduced through parthenogenesis (Andreoni, 2016)
- Healing, particularly poor digestion or headaches

One of the oldest instruments ever discovered, a 35,000-year-old Stone Age flute, was made from the bone of a griffon vulture, so both air and music are also strong associations with these magnificent birds.

Folklore

In some North American First Nations' cultures, the mythical Thunderbird is a great vulture. The bird is a god to some, and large enough to carry an orca away in its talons. Aptly named, the Thunderbird controlled the weather or was at the very least a portent for it. Some tales tell of the Thunderbird producing lightning from its eyes and causing claps of thunder with every beat of its wings. Across different groups of people, the Thunderbird has different meanings. It may be associated with strength, nobility, and the start of summer. Yet some see it as an avenging beast, to be respected but avoided.

Magic

A vulture in your dreams or visualisations can mean you're not looking after yourself well and need to indulge in some self-care. Vultures look after the committee; they're social and protective of their communities. If they're coming to you, they may recognise that you need a prompt to do the right thing for your mental, physical, or emotional well-being.

A Spell for Confidence and Independence

Take a small image of a vulture. You can etch this on a piece of wood if you're artistic or simply print it out on paper. Hold the image. Breathe. See the vulture. It takes what it needs and no more. It shares with its community. It grasps opportunities with both talons, patient but always moving forward. Imagine these qualities in yourself. No matter the setbacks, you can move forward. You can make choices independently of others while still accepting the help and support of your friends, family, or other community.

Place the image in a small bag. Add three small objects that represent something you're proud of. These are the evidence that you've been confident in the past and you can be again. For example, I would use:

- A small shell, to remind me of the wonderful places I've explored.
- A piece of folded paper with words on, to remind me that I make a living as a writer through my own efforts and confidence.
- A small scrap of seasonal herb to remind me that I grow things and understand their benefits, and share that knowledge with others.

It's worth making a note of the objects and why you've used them. This will reinforce the message that you have achieved what you wanted in the past and you *are* capable of doing so again. Tie the bag tightly, and keep it with you or somewhere highly visible to constantly remind you of your own abilities.

I came across another magical and mythological link to the vulture while studying Loki. One of Loki's epithets or kennings (a name he's given in certain contexts and to highlight certain attributes) is Vulture's Path. Loki is sometimes called Loptr, meaning roughly "Air," the literal path of the flying vulture. But I like to think there's more to it than this. Loki is often slated as an agent of chaos, but he's the ultimate mess cleaner. Yeah, okay, he causes plenty of the messes he makes, but he also fixes a wide range of problems, such as ensuring the walls of Asgard aren't built quite in time to cause a major incident, or rescuing Iðunn. Just as vultures gulp down the unsavoury morsels no one else wants, Loki steps up time and again and deals with his own messes and those of others – often at great personal cost.

The vulture is a reminder that we're only one mistake away from having to swallow our pride and do something we'd really rather not. But, also, vultures are a great symbol of personal responsibility and kindness and care for our community.

Chapter 3

Birds of Prey

Sharp wings tug at frigid air
Thermals crippled
By Cailleach's touch.
Though sky is her hue
Delightful deep blue,
Her breath makes the bird
Struggle for height
Strive for flight.
He circles, frustrated,
Almost black against
The colourful morning.
He scars the misty white face
Of the half moon;
A cataract eye
Blinking behind cloud lids;
Tired of night
So drifting sleepily into day.
Music in my ears as this tableau-
Hawk framed by half moon-
Is forever sealed by the kiss
Of blessed memory.

Iðunn now appears for the second time in this book. She is the rejuvenating one; a goddess who is the keeper of the apples of youth and immortality. Note: Although commonly referred to as apples, the fruit of youth could, in fact, be another fruit or even a nut, as *epli*, the word used to describe them in the source material, is used for several types of fruit and nut. Her primary tale is the *Kidnapping of Iðunn* (often anglicised to Idun), in which Loki both causes her to be kidnapped and rescues her.

Odin, Loki, and Hoenir are travelling, and stop to eat after finding and killing an ox. They are hungry, and attempt to cook the meat, but no matter how they try, it won't heat up. A great eagle takes responsibility for this, stating that his magic is stopping the meat from cooking. He agrees to let the meat cook, if he can share the meat. However, once the meat cooks, the eagle takes all the best bits, which angers Loki who finds this unjust. Loki tries to strike the eagle with a branch, but the great bird grasps the branch and flies away with Loki dangling precariously beneath. The eagle reveals his true nature: he is Thjazi, a giant, and will only release Loki if the god promises to bring him the goddess Iðunn and some of her magical fruit.

Loki has no choice but to agree, and upon returning to Asgard, tricks Iðunn into leaving Asgard and her orchard to seek out even more wonderful fruits. Iðunn brings some of her own fruits to compare with the new ones. Thjazi follows and, in his eagle form, snatches Iðunn away to his home, Thrymheim or Thunder Home.

Without Iðunn and her apples, the gods become weak, fragile, old, and infirm. Someone reports that Iðunn was last seen with Loki, and upon pain of death, Loki sets out to rescue the goddess from the dangerous giant. The Goddess Freya has a collection of feathers, perhaps a cloak, that allows the wearer to transform into a falcon. She lends this to Loki, and as a bird of prey, he sets out on his quest. Thjazi is out fishing when Loki arrives at his home, so the god quickly transforms Iðunn into a nut so he can carry her back to Asgard in his talons. Thjazi is, naturally, not happy about this once he discovers Iðunn's escape. His eagle form is much larger and more powerful than Loki's falcon shape. He nearly catches the escapees, but as Loki approaches the walls of Asgard, the other gods pile wood around the walls and light it on fire just as Loki arrives. Loki and Iðunn make it safely over the flames, but the overzealous eagle can't stop before the flames burst higher, and he perishes. (Anderson, 1879).

This story has numerous themes, but the birds here remind us that size and power aren't everything, and that it's okay to have help to achieve the things we need to accomplish. Loki is a powerful shapeshifter and magic user, but he can't become a falcon without Freya's help. The eagle could not have killed the ox on its own – although, of course, a real eagle wouldn't have needed the meat cooking, which should have given the roaming gods a clue as to the bird's real identity!

Despite their power, speed, and ferociousness, each of the birds in this tale of trickery and deception needs help and support from others. It's also worth noting that when the eagle forces the gods to help him, it ends in tragedy and kidnapping. When the gods help Loki and Iðunn willingly, the tale is ended well – although, not for Thjazi, of course! Ultimately, this tale is a reminder that you can be anything you want to be, and reach for any goal, but you don't have to do it alone – and trying to go it alone can actually make things worse, as we see when Loki tries to hide his misdeed of taking Iðunn to Thjazi.

Let's take a look at some of the more notable birds of prey and their magical associations – and don't forget to explore the ones in your local area to find out more.

Eagles

It makes sense to start our brief exploration of birds of prey with eagles, having just heard the tale of Iðunn, Loku, and Thjazi. Eagles have so many different associations across different cultures, and are widely revered in spiritual and magical circles. There are also many, many kinds of eagles. My American readers may first bring to mind the striking bald eagle, *Haliaeetus leucocephalus*, with its white head and striking yellow beak. The national bird of the United States, the bald eagle is classed as one of the ten extant (still in existence) sea eagles. It has a species pair, another bird very similar in many respects, which is the white-tailed eagle (*Haliaeetus albicilla*) that lives across Europe and Asia.

In the UK, the white-tailed eagle is one of the largest birds of prey we have and one of only two "true" eagle species resident in our country. The other is the striking golden eagle, *Aquila chrysaetos*. Once hunted to near extinction, and then harmed further by the reckless use of pesticides, the golden eagle is now making a comeback in Scotland thanks to ongoing conservation efforts.

Correspondences and Associations

- Strength
- Freedom
- Spirituality
- Spiritual balance
- Peace
- Hospitality
- Protection
- Health and healing
- Hunting
- Psychopomp – a being that guides spirits to the afterlife or underworld
- Respecting rules and regulations
- Responsibility and consequences

Folklore

The Pueblo peoples of North America associate eagles with the direction of "Up," connected to balance and spirituality.

In North America, the killing and particularly the eating of eagles is strictly taboo in many cultures. There are some peoples who have specialist Eagle Killers, those with special spiritual permission to hunt eagles. Sometimes, this is only allowed in winter when other food sources are not available. For those who need eagle feathers for medicine or spiritual purposes, the bird must be caught alive and released again once the feather has been plucked. Anyone who eats forbidden eagle meat will be turned into a monster.

The eagle is also an important clan animal in some North American cultures. Tribes with Eagle clans may have their feathers and designs on ceremonial items and totem poles.

There's a Welsh belief that eagles create storms while breeding on Snowdon, the nation's tallest mountain (Tate, 2007).

Magic

Note: There are many North American traditions from First Nations tribes involving the medicine of the eagle. Please don't reproduce these unless you have genuine associations with a tribe or permission from those peoples. Indigenous Americans were banned from practicing their religion until 1978, so to take parts of it and use it without cultural context is potentially offensive and problematic. Throughout the book, while I may mention the cultural significance of birds to First Nations peoples, I try and steer clear of any ritual practices to avoid these eventualities.

Seeing an eagle is always an awesome sight. See how long you can watch an eagle in flight for – is it rising on a thermal, dwindling to a speck in the sky? Or is it hunting, soaring, or diving? The eagle can help train your focus as you learn to pick out and watch these massive yet agile birds. You can call on this focus to help with meditation or other spiritual practices.

Finding an eagle feather means a moment of transformation is coming, or that you may be freed from a situation that's been troubling you. If you have an altar or sacred space, consider cleaning the feather gently and placing it at the east to represent air, the eagle, and your approaching freedom.

Owls

Curl up like the owl
In the day, allergic
To the light
It's salt in the wound
Of apathy, fragile and forced.
Yes, I'm a ghost until dusk
Drifting through life
Until darkness takes
It's hold, so bold
Oh breath! Breathe and release.
My willowy branches
Take a different stance
And again I am the owl
On the hunt; on the prowl.
See my glowing eyes
And fear me.

There are at least 220 species of owls in the world. These
beautiful birds of prey are often all lumped together as being

nocturnal, but there are in fact diurnal (active in the daylight) owls and crepuscular ones that are most active around dusk or dawn.

Owls are famous for their wide range of vision, aided by forward facing eyes and a spine/neck that allows them to rotate their heads 270 degrees to see in nearly every direction.

Many owls can glide silently through the night, giving them a ghost-like presence which, of course, adds to the many folktales and myths surrounding these fascinating birds. The barn owl, *Tyto alba*, is particularly associated with the otherworldly, ghosts, spirits, and omens of death. These spooky associations are helped along by its unearthly, screeching call.

Correspondences and Associations

- Athena
- Peace
- Prosperity
- Olive trees (a connection via the Goddess Athena)
- Wisdom
- Knowledge
- Protection
- Victory
- Death
- Ghosts
- Misfortune
- The sound "M" in Ancient Egyptian hieroglyphs

Folklore

Seeing a nocturnal owl, for example, a barn owl, during the day is supposed to be an omen of severe misfortune. If an owl crashes into your window or the side of your home, this is supposed to mean that death is on the way. Of course, it could just be for the poor, injured bird.

Hearing an owl's shriek during the birth of a child is a portent of doom for that child or the family. However, some beliefs hold that the call of an owl can determine the gender of the child.

In Ancient Rome, if an owl was caught it would be burned and its remains thrown into a river to prevent it alighting on someone's home and foretelling their death.

The Pima people of Arizona have a belief that humans and owls share souls, or that a dying person's soul is carried away by an owl. There is a custom of giving owl feathers to someone who is on their deathbed (Tate, 2007).

Placing garlic around an infant may protect it from the *Strix* or screech owl, who otherwise may feed the child poisoned milk.

Magic
While the folkloric associations with owls are mostly bleak, modern magic can look to the many positive associations with owls.

Owls are determined hunters and quiet, silently progressing their way through the twilight to get what they want. In a similar way, you can set your sights on your goals and, without drama, make the moves needed to get things done.

Finding an owl feather may indicate that you're ready to learn a lesson or, possibly, to go back into education. Owls are the animal of Athena and closely linked to wisdom and learning. If you've been considering retraining, learning something new, or completing a course you never completed, signs from the owl can be a firm indicator that this is a good course of action.

One of the most spectacular things I ever saw was when we were driving to see family in Hornsea. It was dusk, and the land along this particular but of the drive is flat fields lined with short hedgerows. In the dwindling light, I caught a movement in my peripheral vision. I looked out to my left, and flying alongside us was a barn owl, utterly oblivious to our presence and focused on its evening prey. Absolutely stunning.

Peregrine Falcons

When thinking about birds of prey, one of the first that always comes to mind for me is the peregrine falcon, *Falco peregrinus*. I'm fortunate enough to have seen one in flight, performing its world record-breaking dive that can see it reaching speeds of over 200 miles per hour.

Peregrine falcons are about the size of a crow, and very striking with their speckled, white fronts and hooded faces finished with a lethal, yellow and black beak. They're found all over the world, but numbers in the UK dwindled due to human activity – yet again, another victim of needless persecution and the overuse of harmful agricultural chemicals. Peregrine falcons are now a protected species, but unfortunately, some gamekeepers still use illegal poison and traps to kill the birds so they can protect grouse and other birds that are bred just to be shot.

Correspondences and Associations

- Speed
- Agility
- Ferocity
- Aggressiveness
- Warfare
- Mastery over the element of air
- Transformation
- Moving from one state to another
- Gullibility
- The Goddess Brigid via tales of St Brigid
- Perseverance
- Survival
- Tenacity

Folklore

One Irish folktale tells of how a falcon (or hawk) persuaded a crow to teach him all his tricks and techniques so that the falcon could become a better hunter. The crow kept him waiting for two years before explaining the trick that would allow the falcon to attack another bird from beneath. But before the falcon realised what was happening, the crow had demonstrated this trick by killing the falcon (Mac Coitir, 2015).

Some Irish places are named after *Seabhac*, the Irish word for hawk or falcon. A falcon in Kildare, Ireland was once called Brigid's bird and the locals believed that many generations of the falcon's family were the same, long-lived bird (Mac Coitir, 2015).

People of the Southwestern Ceremonial Complex in the Mississippi area of North America have revered the peregrine falcon throughout their history. In these traditions, the falcon is associated with the overworld of light and order, the realm of the sun and the moon. The falcon may also have been a messenger, moving between the overworld and the middleworld (Earth) delivering messages for other spirits and beings.

The Japanese characters for "falcon" when unmodified refer specifically to the peregrine falcon. This word, *hayabusa*, has poetic associations with winter. Suzuki took the term for one of their powerful motorbikes to encapsulate the properties of speed and power.

Magic

When you're in a rush, channel the energy of the peregrine falcon. Not only is it incredibly fast, but when it gets where it's going, it makes a huge impact. Peregrine falcons use a "punch" with one claw powered by all that speed, that can instantly kill their prey. These birds encourage us to "go for the kill," strike while opportunities are hot, and go for what we want without compromise.

Merlins

The bird with the name of a wizard. Surely, that's what everyone thinks when they first hear of the merlin? But which came first – the legend, or the bird? It turns out that the two names are unrelated – the wizard's name Merlin is from the Welsh, Myrddin, whereas the bird's name comes from the Old French word *esmerillon*.

The merlin, *Falco columbarius*, is the UK's smallest bird of prey, and challenging to spot in the wild. It moves seasonally across Eurasia, and is a year-round resident in parts of North America where it's sometimes known as the Pigeon Hawk

Correspondences and Associations

- Magic
- Falconry
- Hunting
- Power
- The element of air
- Bringing order out of chaos
- Dominating others
- Understanding other birds

Folklore

In falconry, a merlin was often considered a "lady's bird", which considering how powerful and accurate a hunter the merlin is, suggests a deeper respect for women than some historical sources would have us believe. Catherine the Great may have hunted with a merlin.

Magic

Dreaming of a merlin may mean that a jumbled situation may be about to come into focus for you. However, it can also mean that you need to approach a problem from a more forceful or assertive position.

Meditate on the merlin for success in career progression. This small yet sturdy bird knows how to go for what it wants and is associated with formal hierarchies, making it a powerful symbol for traditional working environments.

Shrikes

Shrikes are a predatory bird quite unlike any of the others in this chapter. Also known as butcherbirds, these small, finch-like birds have a shocking feeding habit: They impale their prey on spikes. That's right, you can find shrike victims ranging from large insects to small lizards impaled on thorns or barbed wire, which is the shrike's MO.

They do this because, although they have hooked beaks like other birds of prey, they don't have big talons for holding and ripping. So, they utilize any spike they can find to immobilize their prey so they can peck it to bits. If there's no spike available, they'll often use the crook of a tree branch. This technique allows them to hunt prey nearly as large as themselves, including other birds.

Correspondences and Associations

- Adaptability
- Intelligence
- Practicality
- Cannibalism
- Aggression
- Strategic thinking
- Calculated violence
- Strength
- Perseverance
- Hope

Folklore

One piece of Zulu folklore tells of a black and white shrike favoured by the current ruler, King Shaka. The king's warriors called the bird, "Scatterer of Enemies," and, in order to ensure victory, they would wear shrike feathers in their heads and arms. After defeating the enemy, the feathers would be displayed prominently during the subsequent celebrations.

Magic

When would you ever need to channel the fierce, uncompromising nature of the shrike; the butcherbird? While impaling enemies and cannibalism aren't recommended, you can take inspiration from the bird's ability to use what is to hand and to overcome its shortcomings. When you think you *can't*, think about how the shrike handles problems almost as big as itself – and eats them up.

Chapter 4

Water Birds

When we think of birds, it's natural to think of the element of air. After all, most birds fly, and we look up to the sky or the treetops to see them. Yet many birds defy this categorization, and none more so than water birds. From ducks to divers, these beasts are at home on lakes, ponds, or even the oceans as they are in the sky – some even preferring a liquid home.

Ducks

Ducks are, on the surface (pun intended), cute, quacky birds that waggle their tail feathers and dunk themselves in the water to feed. In reality, they're fierce, violent, and horribly rapacious. This is particularly true of the common mallards who are found all over the world. The males have bottle green heads and the females are a speckled brown, each beautiful in their own way. However, their mating habits are anything but beautiful. Both sexes have complex genitalia which means the drakes (males) are capable of forcing female ducks against their will – but females are capable of fighting back or even offloading unwanted sperm, in some cases.

Despite these unsavoury habits, many people enjoy a day out at a pond or lake feeding the ducks, particularly when they have a trail of fluffy, yellow-brown ducklings behind them.

Correspondences and Associations

- Malice
- A hidden dark side
- Family
- Speed and agility

- Divinity
- Fidelity
- Sexual prowess
- Weather divination

Folklore

Pope Gregory IX accused some peasants of devil worship, specifically of fraternising with Asmodeus, who would appear to them in a form of a duck and prompt the locals into sexual orgies. I guess the Pope knew a thing or two about the habits of ducks! (Tate, 2007).

In China, the fat of the mandarin duck has been used as an aphrodisiac.

Magic

The duck is a fantastic parent and has been known to approach humans in distress when a duckling has gone missing. Channel the duck if you need the courage and willpower to advocate for your children in challenging situations.

Ducks stay warm in freezing cold water thanks to a combination of fat, oils, and feathers. Think about how you line your nest and clothe yourself; are you taking care of all your needs? Are you cozy enough in your life, or are you suffering needlessly? Making small changes to your daily comfort can make a big impact on your overall well-being.

Geese

The goose is particularly strong symbol in my life, after a mentor picked it out as a spiritual connection for me. She used a deck of cards and pulled out the goose, and noted its connotations as a bird associated with growing family. The next day, I found out I was pregnant.

So, there was no question about including this waterfowl in this book on bird magic!

In my local area, we have two primary types of wild geese: Canada geese which are largely migratory, although some now stay through the winter, and greylag geese, who will literally follow you home if they think you have food.

Correspondences and Associations

- Having both your head in the air and your feet on the ground
- Ferocity
- Protectiveness and bravery
- Loudness
- Making an entrance
- Adaptability
- Making yourself at home wherever you are
- Relocation
- Moving house
- Family
- Children
- Teamwork

Folklore

If wild, migratory geese arrive on our shores earlier than usual, Irish folklore tells us that this means there is poor or stormy weather ahead (Mac Coitir, 2015).

Goose bones have been found in Scandinavian burial goods, signifying their importance to Northern cultures. It may have been customary at one time to sacrifice geese to Odin around the time of the autumnal equinox (Tate, 2007).

Magic

Opening a group ritual or circle with a large goose feather can imbue the space with a sense of close bonding and renew friendships.

Spotting geese flying in their typical "V" formation is a sight to behold. Watch how as one goose flies forward, another will take their position, as they all look out for each other and their shared goal or destination. The goose is a great reminder that teamwork really does make the dream work.

Swans

The Black Swan
Captured forever on water
Now so still
Then rippling with life
Gifted by wind
Airy heartbeats
Thrumming beneath
Your ebony breast.
Smooth and slow
A stately slide
Across this breathing pond.
Yet beneath the chuckling surface
I know too well
Your legs are tired
Pushing, pulling, forcing back
The endless current.

The swan is a truly majestic figure of a bird. In the UK, they're regarded as royal birds and are, without exception, all owned by the current monarch. When Queen Elizabeth II died in 2022, ownership of the swans passed to King Charles III. While he doesn't actually have to go and look after the stately birds, he can legally claim any swan swimming in open water to do with as he wishes.

As well as being royal subjects, swans are closely linked to humans through the power of transformation. There are multiple tales of people being transformed into swans, enough to fill a book all by themselves. Swan magic is particularly prevalent in Irish tales. Cú Chulainn almost kills a princess who came to him in the shape of a swan. In *Tochmarc Étaine* (The Wooing of Étaine), both Étaine and Midir transform into swans. *Oidheadh Chlainne Lir* (Children of Lir) is possibly one of the most famous examples of swan transformation. A jealous stepmother turns her husband's children into swans and, well, no one gets a happy ending in this tragic tale.

Correspondences and Associations

- Loyalty
- Love
- Transformation
- Protectiveness
- Grace
- Serenity
- Patience
- Royalty

Folklore
It's illegal to kill a swan in the UK, but this prohibition is echoed elsewhere. In Ireland, for example, it's considered very bad luck to harm or kill a swan (Mac Coitir, 2015). Perhaps this is because there is a chance it could be a real person under an enchantment. Three swans on the wing may be an omen of death. However, seeing seven swans at once is a sign that seven years of peace are on the way.

Magic
I'm lucky enough to have a huge swan feather which was gifted to me by a very magical friend of mine who now lives in South America. She carefully attached the feather to a keyring so I

could hang it wherever I liked. It's currently hung above my Hekate altar by the front door – although there's no direct link between this powerful Titan Goddess and swans that I'm aware of. However, She is a goddess of liminal spaces, and often guards the boundaries of things. Swans are also protective, and this feels like the right place to have this gift; a connection between friends who are worlds apart, and a link to a bird of both the air and the water between us.

If you are lacking creativity or suffering from artist's or writer's block, consider meditating on the swan. You may find that this elegant yet fierce bird brings the transformative mindset you need to step back onto your creative path.

Penguins

There are at least 18 distinct species of penguins and, contrary to popular media, they don't all live in cold and frosty climes. Galapagos penguins, for example, are tiny (just 14 inches tall) and fairly happy in their tropical environment. However, they are in trouble, as climate change is causing their food – fish and crustaceans – to move further from the islands they call home.

Now, getting their next meal is a dangerous and potentially deadly journey out to sea (Kelly, 2023).

Because penguins generally live in places where not many humans reside, they can seem unusually "friendly," but of course, they simply don't recognise us as a threat. This leads to us seeing them as cute, almost cuddly beasts, which is reinforced by their waddling gait and mannerisms. However, watch one of these birds dive into the water and swim, and you're in the presence of pure grace. I've watched these birds in awe so many times and know they are to be respected and revered as perfect examples of adaptation to extreme circumstances and environments.

Correspondences and Associations

- Something being perfectly suited to its environment
- Grace
- Agility
- Family
- Love
- Queer romance, love, and sexuality (penguins will quite happily form same-sex couples)
- Gift giving

Folklore

A dreamtime story from Australia tells of *Jeedara*, the great white whale, who swam with the penguin and other animals as he went on a journey to protect the oceans and teach other beings the ways of creation. During the adventure, *Djulea*, the penguin, was burnt by fire. The resulting red and yellow markings turned him into the emperor penguin. Other versions of this tale state that *Jeedara* is a great serpent, which is what the artist has depicted near our picture of a penguin at the start of this chapter.

Magic

Penguins give rocks to each other to indicate that they'd like to start building a nest together. And no, those memes saying penguins spend hours or days searching for the perfect pebble aren't true. Real penguins wouldn't have time for that! Consider how you can show someone that you want to start a bond with them. This doesn't have to be romantic. It could be a new work relationship, a fun project, or even starting a band together. Sometimes, it's okay to make the first move and give your pal a rock.

Chapter 5

More Famous Birds in Mythology and Folklore

As this is such a short, introductory volume, it's not possible to include the rich wealth of magical birds that I've encountered in my travels and my research. However, I think the following feathery friends need a special mention.

Roadrunners

Remember the Roadrunner and Wile E. Coyote cartoons? I loved those growing up. Roadrunner was so fast, agile, and smart – and it turns out, not so far removed from his real-life inspiration.

The actual roadrunner is incredibly fast and quite large – up to two feet in both length and wingspan. This striking member of the cuckoo family lives in dry, arid places, and often forgoes flight (except for the odd short burst) in favour of running at high speeds and for long distances. They're also surprisingly fierce, being one of the few birds that can take down rattlesnakes. The roadrunner only resides in the Americas, largely in the south of the United States, Mexico, and Central America. Unsurprisingly, the roadrunner's influence appears in many First Nations tales.

Correspondences and Associations

- Ferocity
- Protection
- Speed
- Agility
- Parenting, protecting children
- Stamina
- Freedom
- Luck

Folklore

One Apache legend tells the tale of how the roadrunner became the leader of all birds. Unlike the Oriole, the roadrunner was not too quiet. Unlike the mockingbird, he wasn't too loud. Unlike the bluejay, he wasn't too proud or vain. And, the other birds reasoned, the roadrunner is so fast he can get to meetings quicker than anyone! A great example of how balance combined with a unique talent can take you far (Canku Ota, 2003).

Magic

Some First Nation peoples believe that the roadrunner is a spirit messenger and a guide to find your way home. If you are lost or unsure of what path to take in your life, consider meditating on the roadrunner. You may find the guidance you are looking for.

Pigeons and Doves

Humans used to have a much closer relationship with pigeons than we do today. As far back as 1350 BCE, people were using pigeons as messengers, relying on their innate homing instincts to trust that they would always come back. During the 19th Century, these techniques were adopted by the military and became a major aspect of strategic warfare.

Julius G. Neubronner, was the son of a pharmacist with a passion for photography. In 1907 he patented the design of a unique camera tailored for pigeons. The idea was that the pigeon would fly and the camera would automatically take pictures, thus providing a pictorial account of the bird's journey. The camera was a big hit for a few years, used by scientists, journalists, and even for military applications. However, as the use of pigeons fell out of favour, this awesome invention was also consigned to the history books. However, it's an incredible reminder of how closely humans and birds can collaborate when inspired.

Correspondences and Associations

- Innovation
- Always knowing your way home
- Trust
- Partnership
- Exploitation
- Aphrodite
- Death
- Luck, both good and bad
- Divination and oracles
- Speaking up for oneself
- Peace
- New beginnings

Folklore

Doves are generally known as birds of peace; the bearer of the olive branch at the end of the flood. The great thing about researching this book was finding juxtapositions to commonly held beliefs. I found today, that in some Southern American States, the sound of doves cooing was thought to portent bad luck or black magic. Furthermore, one should not chase the birds away, as this may anger the witch or evil spirit who has sent them.

The Journal of American Folklore tells us that wood pigeons are a sign of either ill or good fortune – not very helpful, I grant you! Apparently the sounds a pigeon or dove makes will foretell the outcome of your endeavours. Sadly, it's not clear which sounds herald good news and which bad.

Another tale tells of how a wood pigeon 'wailed' whilst Jesus was dying on the cross, trying to alleviate his agony with its song. Yet another story states that if a pigeon lands on your house, someone you know is going to die.

Magic

Give a dove or pigeon feather to someone you want to build bridges with. Just remember to clean any bird poo off it first!

Watch a flock of pigeons take off from a city roof. See how they circle and land again. Do they all stay together? Does the shape of the flock in flight remind you of anything?

Hummingbirds

Here is another bird I have only seen in books and pictures. But oh, how wish I had! The videos I've seen of people with nectar-filled feeders and the resulting visiting hummingbirds give me the biggest bird envy. These tiny birds are incredible, with the largest growing over six inches in length but the smallest barely two inches long! This latter beast, the bee hummingbird (*Mellisuga helenae*) is usually only found in Cuba, and is classed as both the smallest bird *and* smallest dinosaur ever recorded, because nothing similar in either type of creature has ever been found that's quite as diminutive. So, for the many ornithologists and scientists that recognise that birds are, in fact, avian dinosaurs, yes, this hummingbird is the world's tiniest one.

Hummingbirds can fly in any direction, including backwards, with their combined light-weight and their super-fast wings providing them with incredible acrobatic abilities. However, to sustain this power, they have to eat the nectar of up to 2,000 flowers every day.

Correspondences and Associations

- Hunger
- Industriousness
- Agility
- Perseverance
- Activity, being on the go
- Travel, long journeys
- Relocation
- Migration
- Speed
- Physical power
- Good things come in small packages

Folklore

First Nations people in British Columbia state that the thunderbird is similar to the ruby-throated hummingbird. This connection could be to do with the relatively loud sound made by the fast wings of the hummingbird (Armstrong, 1958).

Some other Indigenous peoples of North America believe that the hummingbird brought tobacco to America from the West Indies.

Magic

Is there a better symbol for hard work than the hummingbird? Perhaps the bee, but that's a chapter for another book. This industrial bird is the perfect symbol for keeping going, perseverance, or simply giving it a little more than you even thought you had.

Meditate on the hummingbird to find your drive, your ambition, and focus your efforts in the direction that will yield the best results.

Sparrows

Sparrows live all over the world and can be found in most gardens or yards. The house sparrow, *Passer domesticus*, live close to humans, making use of our buildings and gardens as nesting habitats. However, the RSBP (Royal Society for the Protection of Birds) notes that numbers are in steep decline and have dropped 71% since 1977. It could be that the changing methods of urbanisation and the increase of industrial and commercial sites rather than houses with gardens has had an impact on their numbers.

While today we puzzle over the mystery of dwindling sparrow numbers, in the 18th and 19th centuries, people were hired to kill them in huge numbers as they reportedly did extreme damage to crops.

Correspondences and Associations

- Industriousness
- Community
- Teamwork
- Socialisation
- Class division
- Joy
- Luck
- Endings
- Psychopomps

Folklore

In some parts of China, a sparrow flying into the house is a sign that good luck is on the way.

A sparrow flying into a window can symbolise either death or the ending of something major in your life.

Sparrows may carry the souls of the dead in the role of psychopomp. Stephen King notably made use of this tradition in his 1989 novel, *The Dark Half*, in which he used the birds as agents of death.

Magic

A flock of sparrows in your garden is a sign of good luck for you *and* the environment. Encourage sparrows by leaving seeds out for them or growing bushes with berries on. We have a firethorn bush in the garden, which has stunning white blossoms in early summer and scarlet berries later in the year. We often see sparrows literally hanging off the slender, spiky branches eating their fill of the berries.

Cuckoos

The cuckoo is an enigma. It's a large, beautiful bird whose call heralds the start of spring. Yet every cuckoo's life starts with the death of another family of birds. Cuckoos lay their eggs in other birds' nests. Once the young cuckoo hatches, it monopolises the parents' attention, takes most of the food, and eventually pushes the other baby birds out of the nest. A bleak start to life, to be sure.

According to *The Folklore of Birds*, the cuckoo is expected on different dates around the world, often associated with local spring fairs or feasts. In England, where I live, the cuckoo should be heard around the 14th of April (Armstrong, 1958).

Correspondences and Associations

- Deceit, misdirection, and trickery
- Intelligence

- Opportunism
- Spring
- New beginnings
- Ruthlessness
- Family
- Fertility

Folklore

The cuckoo has so much folklore attached to it, but here are a few snippets:

- An alternative name for the cuckoo is "rain-crow" as its call is supposed to herald a downpour.
- Upon hearing the call of a cuckoo (which sounds exactly like *Cuck-oo*) if you dig up the earth from exactly under your right foot, you gain a magical flea repellent (Pliny, 77-79).
- Look under your shoe if you hear a cuckoo and you will find a hair the same colour as the one you will fall in love with.
- Cuckoos can predict the profitability of the farming season, with one English rhyme stating:

When the cuckoo comes to the bare thorn,
Sell your cow and buy your corn
But when she comes to the full bit
Sell your corn and buy your sheep (Armstrong, 1958)

In other words, an early cuckoo means it's time to invest in agriculture, while a late cuckoo suggests investing in pastoral animals.

Magic

If you have cuckoos near where you live or can travel to some woods to hear them, keep a question in your heart and listen out for their calls. The number of calls you hear will help you find your answer. This could be a measurement of time, how many times you should do something, or the rhythm of the calls may speak to you in a different way.

Starlings

Starlings are dark birds at first glance, but a closer look shows that they're speckled with paler blotches all over. Their feathers are also highly iridescent, which means that when they catch the light, you can see many colours like blues and greens. Starlings are here all year round, although we may see more in winter as some migrate from Eastern Europe. Look out for "murmurations" of starlings; huge clouds of flying starling that seem to swirl and make strange shapes in the sky.

In Britain and Ireland, the starling is prevalent across towns and suburbs, although numbers have dwindled in recent years (Middleton, 2019). As with all things that seem "common," it's easy to overlook the incredible beauty and intelligence of this social, striking bird.

Correspondences and Associations

- Music
- Education
- Family
- Curiosity
- Mimicry
- Disguise
- Communication
- The safe relay of messages
- Secrecy
- Hidden beauty
- Change
- Intuition

Folklore

Starlings are excellent mimics – ones local to us mimic a neighbour whistling, and (more annoyingly) a car alarm! In the *Mabinogion*, a starling is used as a messenger by Branwen, to tell her brother, King Brân, where she was imprisoned. The starling memorises the message and relays it to Brân.

Magic

You may meditate on an image of a starling if you're having communication difficulties with someone. If a starling were to take your words and mimic them, they would be repeated exactly as you spoke them, with the correct intent. Focus on this aspect of starlings to ensure you have the right words to hand before starting a challenging conversation.

Starlings are stunning, iridescent and glimmering in even the barest hint of sunshine. Yet in the shade, they can appear dull and brown. Use this as a reminder that not all beauty is obvious, and even the simplest things can be packed with wonder.

Chapter 6

Birds in Seasonal and Everyday Magic

That first wind of spring
Not the cold whip of January,
Snapping and howling between
Long silent frosts
Neither the pranking pounce
Of February
Still Cailleach gripped
Strong
Eye watering and coat belting
Shuddering down the street
Pulverising the shore
Testing trees and fences alike
No, instead,
The crossover between March winds
And April showers
The promise of later flowers
A green breath,
A great God's sigh
A huff of merry laughter at the sight:
Daffodils, Persephone's lure (or gift)
Bowing not breaking in the breeze
A warm sigh of self-satisfaction
At the birds,
The see-saw sound of great tits
Territorial opera of blackbirds
Lilting whistles of starlings.
I tip my head back
Let divinity breathe

Its green grassy wind
Across my winter-tired eyes.

However you practice magic, whether you consider yourself a witch or simply a spiritual person with an appreciation for the unexplained, you can use your connection to birds to make meaningful changes in your life.

For this next section, I've written four seasonal rituals incorporating birds that are in my local area. You can adapt these to your own needs by:

- Changing the birds to ones more familiar to you.
- Incorporating aspects of your faith, spirituality, or Pagan path.
- Including prayers or devotional material to deities of your choice.
- Holding the ritual at a significant time, for example, you might hold the spring ritual at or around the time of the spring equinox.

When you do these rituals, prepare for them as you would any sacred task according to your path. If you like to ritually cleanse before a ritual, that's perfectly valid here, as is lighting incense or candles (safely, of course). These ritual texts are designed to inspire and you don't need to adhere to them rigidly.

A Bird Ritual for Spring

This ritual celebrates the coming new life of spring and reminds participants to prepare for the year ahead by remembering what is important to them.

You will need:

- The below text
- A seed of your choice and something to plant it in

- A feather, fan, or brush
- Bird food suitable for your local spring birds

Prepare yourself for sacred work as you normally would. For me, this means clean clothes, a nice smell or homemade incense, a quiet space, and three, calming breaths. Ideally, start this ritual inside and move outside after the sweeping. If you can't manage this, don't worry! It will still be as effective.

Ritual Text

Now is the time of greening
Hear the mistle thrush call
Calling back the light
Pushing back the night

Hail to the green,
Buds small and frail
Soon to grow wild
Hearty and hail

Listen to blackbirds
Proud on the edge
Shouting the world down
From every hedge

See the great crow
With her beak full of sticks
Nesting and building
A life for her chicks

Sweep now our homes
Sweep out the cold

Sweep out the hurt
Sweep out the winter

[At this point, use your fan, feather, or brush and visualise sweeping out any negative energies or residual wintery vibes that you want to be rid of. Move your sweeping toward the back door or window of your home, if possible, and head outside once finished, if you can.]

I have swept this space clean
I am ready for spring
I am ready for new life
From this place to bring

Hope, health, and joy.

[Pause, breathe, and plant your seed. Take a moment to imagine it growing with the season, and visualise something you want to grow in your own life.]

As the mistle thrush calls in spring, I too will call to the things
I need in my life.
As the blackbird marks its territory loudly, I too will set
meaningful boundaries.
As the crow builds and nurtures its space, I too will nurture
that which I wish to have more of.

[At this point, if you're inspired to, you could write down anything that comes up in terms of plans and goals for the coming season, or changes you wish to make.]

I am grateful for the calling, singing, building birds
I am grateful for the turning season

I am grateful for the cold and rain as much as the sun and
coming warmer days
For everything has its place.

Now is the time of greening
Hear the mistle thrush call
Calling back the light
Pushing back the night
Reminding us all
The smallest beasts have might.

[Leave food out as offerings to your birds – try and use a raised feeder to help birds avoid attacks from predators. Close your ritual space as you normally would.]

A Bird Ritual for Summer

This ritual is a moment of refreshment in the hottest season and a reminder of the connection other creatures have to us and the elements.

You will need:

- The following ritual text
- Some water

Prepare yourself as you usually would. Be mindful that if the weather is very warm, ritual clothing like heavy robes may need to be sacrificed in the name of comfort and wellbeing. This ritual includes repetitive phrases that work best when chanted a little louder on each turn around to build energy. You can use this text in a group setting to make it even more impactful.

Ritual Text

The heron soaring overhead
Binding air to water, air to water, air to water
While the red breast robin pecks at the hardened ground
Binding earth to fire, earth to fire, earth to fire

Let us rest in that in-between space
Caught between elements
Suspended in mystery
Wondering at the weirdness of our world

We are children of spring,
Growing up in summer
Hot, and in need of rest
Like our feathered friends

Let us drink [take a drink of water]

Let us offer to the Earth [pour water on bare earth, if possible, concrete or asphalt is fine]

Let us offer to the birds that we revere [fill a raised bird bath – birds are often in dire need of water at this time of year]

We pause, we are refreshed
We are ready to move once the heat of summer has passed
We pause, we are invigorated
We are ready to plan and share ambitions
We pause, we are motivated
We are one step closer to knowing who we are and what we want

[This is a great opportunity to add in your own ritual elements such as deity offerings or commitments. Then, after a pause for reflection, it's time to close your ritual space in your usual manner.]

The swan furiously stamping on the surface of the lake
Freed from water to air, water to air, water to air
The swallow's burning breast skimming the dusk
Freed from fire to earth, from fire to earth, from fire to earth

We/I are/am grateful for the gifts of the birds, by the height of
the sun or the light of the summer moon.

A Bird Ritual for Autumn/Fall

This ritual acknowledges the dual nature of autumn – things are dying back but there is beauty all around. It focuses on increasing resilience and sharing what we have with those that we appreciate.

You will need:

- A local seed, e.g., I use an acorn or a horse chestnut (conker)
- A fallen feather if possible – a leaf will do, if this is unattainable
- The following ritual text
- Food suitable for your local birds

Prepare yourself as you normally would.

Ritual Text

The wheel turns again
The leaves fall
While evergreens

Stand bright and tall
And the pheasant croaks
And the starling chatters
While the season chills
And the first frost shatters.

I take this gift from the Earth
Grown with the blessing of the rain
In the light of the summer sun
Fallen through cold air
Into my hand.

[Hold your seed tightly.]

I am grateful for nature's gifts
And will give back when I can
A little water
A little food
Gifts to the land
And the feathered creatures of air.

Now is the time to store food for the dark months
So I will keep this gift I have been given.
Now is the time to honour those close to me
So I will appreciate this gift I have been given.
Now is the time to share with those who have less
And in that spirit, I hold tight then give away
This gift given to me by nature.

[Hold the seed tight, take a moment to appreciate its beauty or how magical it is, then either give to someone in the moment or pick someone you know will appreciate it, then set it aside. In a group setting, you could each pass your seeds to the person on your left.]

This is the darkening of the world
Yet we stand in so much beauty
With swifts soaring southward
And blackbirds hunkering down
Confident that the land will provide.

[Hold your leaf or feather high then let it fall to the floor. Leave it here until the area is closed down after your ritual practice.]

Let us remember this is the time of the great fall
Things die, things rest, and things move away
Be sad in the moment
But happy for the continued turn of the season
The warmth that will come again
And the privilege to gather beloved things close.

[Put out food suitable for your local birds.]

Thank you for your presence in our lives
Social birds
Resilient birds
Noisy birds
Quiet birds
Your diversity is inspiring
A place for everyone
May I make the same accommodations
For myself and those who matter in my life.

[Close your ritual space down as usual.]

A Bird Ritual for Winter

This ritual acknowledges that winter is hard for many and imbues the participants with the desire to look out for each other and their wider community.

You will need:

- An ice cube/piece of ice and a small receptacle
- The following ritual text

Once you've prepared yourself for ritual or sacred working, place your ice in a small dish and place it somewhere in your vicinity. If there are a few of you working together, each take a piece of ice and put it in a central receptacle. The ice will thaw throughout the ritual and after, representing the temporary nature of winter. Once the ice has fully melted, dispose of it safely. If you let it warm up to room temperature, you can water any houseplants you might have with it. Alternatively, simply dispose of it in the garden or yard. Note: Don't pour it over an outdoor walkway, because if it freezes, it may become a fall hazard.

I haven't included a note to feed the birds here, but it's recommended that you leave food and water out for birds throughout winter. Because our homes take up space where their food once grew, many birds struggle to find enough to eat in winter. Supplementing their diet with seeds, dried mealworms, or protein-rich fat balls can help preserve the population of garden birds.

Ritual Text
[Place ice in receptacle.]

> *Now we stand in the dark of the year*
> *Moving both away from and toward the light*
> *Caught in this moment*
> *Of reflection*
>
> *Let us pause and acknowledge*
> *The great black crow fighting blustery winter winds*

Whirling but striving ever forward
Feathers torn and chilled
Yet later groomed to perfection
Taking the rest they need
With their mates.

Can we do the same?
Can we fight for what we need?
Rest when required
Looking out for our tribe —
Those who matter,
Those who would fight for us
Or those who cannot fight at all —
As magic workers,
Can it be our responsibility to look after those who need a little
more
In this cold quarter of the year?

[Each participant of the ritual must reflect on this for themselves
– this is a personal moment.]

Winter is cold and beautiful
Hard and bright
Like a diamond
Let us bypass the shiny objects
Avoid corvid temptation
And search for sustenance
Among the woodland
Of chilly days and nights.

We will learn from the resilience
Of the robin, defending its supplies
Calling its cousins from the continent
Banding together

Foraging in groups
Leaving no one behind.

We drive through the winter as one
We work through the darkness together
We remember the heat of the sun
Even in the iciest weather [repeat this verse three times]

May we be the sheltering wing
May we be the cozy down
May we be the beak that feeds
For those that need it this season.

[Close ritual space as normal, dispose of melted ice as described at the start of this ritual.]

Meditating with Birds

Meditation is a tricky subject for many. Not everyone can meditate in the ways they've been taught are the "right" methods to follow. I'm here to tell you, there's no such thing as the "right" way to meditate. In fact, there are dozens, maybe even hundreds of different ways to meditate. So, while I'm going to outline some brief visualization techniques, if these don't work for you, *do not* beat yourself up. Here are just a few myths and misconceptions about meditation:

- Myth #1 – Everyone can visualize: No, they can't. Aphantasia, the inability to see images in your mind, affects at least 1% of the population (Zeman, 2024).
- Myth #2 – You must count your breaths: Again, no. Some people find this enormously useful. However, others, particularly some neurodivergent people, can find it distressing to focus on their breath. If it doesn't relax you, it has no part in your meditation practice.

- Myth #3 – All meditation is silent: Rarely, if ever. Most people I know use some sort of sound to help focus their busy minds, from gentle music to talking to soundscapes such as ocean noises or, unsurprisingly, bird song.
- Myth #4 – In order to meditate, your mind must be blank: Absolutely not. In fact, if you're striving for this practically unattainable goal, the chances are you're not getting the real benefits of meditation at all. Yes, your mind should be calmer. But no one really ever has a blank mind.

So, what are effective ways to meditate? You can use an app that talks you down into a relaxed headspace. I use Calm and Insight Timer, and the latter has many free tracks that you can stream or download to your computer or smart device. I find noise-cancelling headphones useful during the day, and a sleep-band (soft fabric with flat headphones built-in) essential for nights. You can also focus on a real or virtual candle flame; listen to music; chant; drum; some people even manage to achieve a meditative state while walking or running.

When meditating on birds, you can try and visualise the bird if that's possible for you. Think about its physical appearance; its colour, size, and plumage. What type of beak does it have? Can you see it, or can you imagine what it might feel like? If it landed on you, would it be heavy, or light?

Now, think about the personality of the bird. It may be fast, agile, and adaptable – like the roadrunner. Maybe it's a sneaky one, like the cuckoo. Or perhaps it's a superior hunter, like the peregrine falcon.

Once you've nailed down its attributes, now it's time to think about what the bird means to you magically or spiritually. You can use the correspondences from this book, from your own research, or your own experience. I often think about the jackdaw and its connection to family; its loyalty and intelligence, the huge flocks it forms, and how they all look out for each other.

When you've spent time meditating on birds, try and record your feelings and thoughts afterwards. A bird meditation journal can help you note any patterns and discover new correspondences and magical associations that are unique to your personal relationship with birds.

A Short Visualisation for Working with Birds

[You can record this to play to yourself as you meditate or relax, or simply read it a few times until you are familiar with the scene. If you can't visualise, simply follow the above steps and think about your birds and the places you might see them.]

As you relax, with your eyes closed, you feel warm, safe, and unbothered by everyday concerns. They're still there, but you don't need to deal with them right now.

Inside your mind, you open your eyes. You're on a woodland path. There's the smell of rich earth in the air. Plants grow right up to the edges of the path, and a few feet away, tall trees reach up to the sunlight. You don't move for a moment, simply taking in the wood which mimics the season in real life.

What plants can you see? Try and remember, as these may have some significance.

Once you've had your fill of experiencing this pause on a woodland path, start to move forward. It doesn't matter how you move – do what feels comfortable. As you move, it's as if the woods come alive around you. You can hear the wind gently rustling the trees or grasses. You can also hear bird calls – can you recognise the call? Is it a bird you already know?

After some time, you come to the edge of a clearing in the woods. You instinctively know that, while you will end up in the clearing, you need to wait. You come to a gentle stop. The bird song or call is louder. In the clearing there is a large stone with something on top. As you look, the bird you heard flies down, landing on the stone. It pecks at what you now see is some food. Can you tell what type of bird it is? If you've never seen it before, could you describe it to someone else? What is it eating? Don't feel panicked to retain this information, simply notice what you can and let it become a part of your experience.

Wait for the bird to eat its fill then fly away. As it does, you hear its call again, then there is silence. In that silence, you move slowly into the clearing. There is a feeling of great relaxation. You touch the stone. You may also lean against it or sit by it as you choose. Notice the feel of the stone and the temperature. Also take note of how this makes you feel.

Simply be in this space, and notice that after a few moments, the sounds of the woodland start back up again. You can hear the breeze in the branches again, and various bird and small animal sounds. Nothing is distinct; it's like a gentle, nature-based soundscape. Once you have enjoyed this space for as long as you need, turn and leave the clearing.

Walk back down the path to the point you first remember seeing. In your mind, close your eyes and relax. In reality, open your eyes, and rest a moment with the experiences you just had.

[At this point, it's always a good idea to stretch, move in a way that's comfortable for you, and drink some water. Try and make a note of anything that stood out for you in this meditation, and connect to the spiritual meaning of the bird you saw. With repetition, you may find patterns and messages within your bird meditations.]

Everyday Bird Magic

These are some basic bird-related moments of magic you can give yourself every day.

If you find a feather, take a moment to either examine it with your eyes or pick it up. Some people are nervous about picking feathers up from the ground due to germs and other contaminants, and that's totally fine. I will pick them up if they're not totally gross – sometimes we see the feathers of a small bird caught by a predator, and they're often blood-stained which is not very appealing. However, I often find jackdaw, crow, and magpie feathers which usually make their way onto my altar or other special places. I have a small pigeon feather in the car, stuck in the sun visor. This was a gift from one of my kids, and it won't move from there now. It's my good luck charm for travel – a literal wing and a prayer.

If you notice a small, white feather blowing on the wind, stop and take a moment and think if anyone comes to mind. There are two phenomena I've noticed here: One, that you'll think of a living person and they'll contact you later that day, or you'll realise you need to contact them. Two, you'll remember someone who has died, and you'll get a very strong sense that they're guarding, guiding, or simply being present in some way. You don't have to believe in the afterlife or otherworld for this to be true. In a very real sense, our ancestors, mentors, and other people close to us have ways of guiding us simply by us having experienced their presence in our lives. The feather is a point of connection; a spiritual reminder from your conscience that you have lessons from that person which may apply in your current circumstances.

If a bird relieves itself on your car or other vehicle, try and resist washing it away immediately. Take a moment to thank the bird for its "blessing."

When you see magpies, nod your head and greet them, even if silently. Count them, and decide for yourself what this number means. You can use a traditional rhyme, but you don't have to take it literally. Silver or Gold, for example, could mean something to do with the magical associations of those colours.

Silver can be connected to enhanced intuition, while gold may mean an increased awareness of otherworldly beings.

If you hear a thrush or cuckoo before you leave the house, always take an umbrella with you – just in case.

And remember, every time you feed the birds, it's a simple way of leaving offerings to tiny spirits that can help your life in so many ways.

Time to Roost...

As we come to the end of this short introductory volume, it's my wish that you're inspired to learn more. Throughout the bibliography you can see the books and resources that I used to ensure my scientific facts were up to date – but that shouldn't be the be all and end all of your research.

To get to know the birds, you really need to spend time with them. From a lengthy walk in the woods to simply sitting by an open window, listening to their chatter and songs, there are so many ways for you to connect to these amazing creatures.

Very few other groups of creatures move across the elements of water, air, and earth so effortlessly. There are bats, of course – and how I love those too! And there are the many, many insects that feed so many of the birds we've looked at in this volume. But none are as visible as the birds; as beautiful, resilient, magical, awe-inspiring, and woven throughout folklore and mythology all over the world.

Research which birds are common to your local area and keep an eye out for them. Consider dedicating a journal to your bird-discovery efforts. It doesn't need to be full-time bird watching, but you may find that as you learn more about your feathery neighbours, you turn into an amateur ornithologist very quickly!

Above all, note how each of these creatures makes you feel; associations, correspondences, and other points that can help you hone your own personal magic practice. Always start with the lore – folktales, religious or spiritual connections, or mythology. From here, it's possible to start building your own catalogue of magical correspondences. Just remember, if you share these, make sure others know that these are your own musings rather than sourced from somewhere else. This helps other bird fans create their own relationship to birds rather than simply trying to emulate yours.

A final word from one of my favourites that I simply didn't have the space to cover in this book: The curlews, a wading bird that comes inland to nest, with a haunting, whooping call that sounds like the manifestation of magic itself:

The Curlews, They Are Calling
Nothing moves me more than their call
Whooping joyfully over the tents
Winding up over and over
A perpetual toy helicopter
Always on the verge of either
Taking off or landing
The beating wings so fierce
So fast
Then soaring effortlessly
While their ghost cries fill the
Grey afternoon.
Then comes the night
Oyster catchers fly purposefully north east
Heading for the coast
Chasing the low tide
Yet the curlew still roams
Perhaps she's guarding her nest
Perhaps she's talking to a neighbour
Perhaps she's just out doing bird errands
Humans can't fathom.

The curlew swoops, night-cloaked and haunting
Joyfully spiralling upward in tone
Calling me to linger
Calling me to wonder
Calling me to see.

Bibliography

Anderson, R. B. (1879). Translation of The Younger Edda: Also Called Snore's Edda, or The Prose Edda. S. C. Griggs and Company.

Andreoni, M. (2016). Vultures: Exegesis Of A Symbol. Journal of Ancient History and Archaeology, 3(4). https://doi.org/10.14795/j.v3i4.204

Armstrong, E. A. (1958). The Folklore of Birds. Collins.

Chadd, R.W; Taylor, M. (2016) Birds: Myth, Lore and Legend. Bloomsbury.

Egan, L. B. (1988) A Christmas Stocking: A Child's Treasury for the Festive Season. Simon & Schuster Ltd.

Elder, Pliny The. (79). Naturalis Historia. Pliny the Elder.

Kelly, D. B. (2023, January 25). These are the Penguins that Don't Live in the Cold. Grunge. Retrieved May 26, 2024, from https:// www.grunge.com/314899/these-are-the-penguins-that-dont-live-in-the-cold/

Mac Coitir, N. (2015). Ireland's Birds: Myths, Legends and Folklore. The Collins Press.

Meyer, K. (1904) Revue Celtique.

Middleton, K. (2019, January 1). The decline of British starlings. Birdwatch.

Opie, I.; Tatem, M. (1989) A Dictionary of Superstitions. Oxford University Press.

Ota, C. (n.d.). How Roadrunner Became the Leader of the Birds. Canku Ota. http://www.cankuota.org/IssueHistory/Issues03/Co08092003/CO_08092003_Roadrunner.htm

Roth, S. (2022, May 25). The Most Musical Songbirds in America. Birds&Blooms. Retrieved May 30, 2024, from https://www.birdsandblooms.com/birding/bird-species/songbirds/top-songbirds-america/

Stratton, F. Reid, B. M. (1936) When the Storm God Rides. Charles Scribner's Sons.

Tate, P. (2007). Flights of Fancy. Random House.

Zeman, A. (2024). Aphantasia and hyperphantasia: Exploring imagery vividness extremes. Trends in Cognitive Sciences. https://doi.org/10.1016/j.tics.2024.02.007

MOON BOOKS
PAGANISM & SHAMANISM

What is Paganism? A religion, a spirituality, an alternative belief system, nature worship? You can find support for all these definitions (and many more) in dictionaries, encyclopaedias, and text books of religion, but subscribe to any one and the truth will evade you. Above all Paganism is a creative pursuit, an encounter with reality, an exploration of meaning and an expression of the soul. Druids, Heathens, Wiccans and others, all contribute their insights and literary riches to the Pagan tradition. Moon Books invites you to begin or to deepen your own encounter, right here, right now.

If you have enjoyed this book, why not tell other readers by posting a review on your preferred book site.

Bestsellers from Moon Books

Keeping Her Keys
An Introduction to Hekate's Modern Witchcraft
Cyndi Brannen
Blending Hekate, witchcraft and personal development
together to create a powerful new magickal perspective.
Paperback: 978-1-78904-075-3 ebook 978-1-78904-076-0

Journey to the Dark Goddess
How to Return to Your Soul
Jane Meredith
Discover the powerful secrets of the Dark Goddess and
transform your depression, grief and pain into healing
and integration.
Paperback: 978-1-84694-677-6 ebook: 978-1-78099-223-5

Shamanic Reiki
Expanded Ways of Working with Universal Life Force Energy
Llyn Roberts, Robert Levy
Shamanism and Reiki are each powerful ways of healing; together,
their power multiplies. Shamanic Reiki introduces techniques to
help healers and Reiki practitioners tap ancient healing wisdom.
Paperback: 978-1-84694-037-8 ebook: 978-1-84694-650-9

Southern Cunning
Folkloric Witchcraft in the American South
Aaron Oberon
Modern witchcraft with a Southern flair, this book is a
journey through the folklore of the American South and
a look at the power these stories hold for modern witches.
Paperback: 978-1-78904-196-5 ebook: 978-1-78904-197-2

Bestsellers from Moon Books
Pagan Portals Series

The Morrigan
Meeting the Great Queens
Morgan Daimler

Ancient and enigmatic, the Morrigan reaches out to us.
On shadowed wings and in raven's call, meet the ancient Irish
goddess of war, battle, prophecy, death, sovereignty, and magic.
Paperback: 978-1-78279-833-0 ebook: 978-1-78279-834-7

The Awen Alone
Walking the Path of the Solitary Druid
Joanna van der Hoeven

An introductory guide for the solitary Druid, The Awen Alone
will accompany you as you explore, and seek out your
own place within the natural world.
Paperback: 978-1-78279-547-6 ebook: 978-1-78279-546-9

Moon Magic
Rachel Patterson

An introduction to working with the phases of the Moon,
what they are and how to live in harmony with the lunar
year and to utilise all the magical powers it provides.
Paperback: 978-1-78279-281-9 ebook: 978-1-78279-282-6

Hekate
A Devotional
Vivienne Moss

Hekate, Queen of Witches and the Shadow-Lands,
haunts the pages of this devotional bringing magic
and enchantment into your lives.
Paperback: 978-1-78535-161-7 ebook: 978-1-78535-162-4

Readers of ebooks can buy or view any of these bestsellers by clicking on the live link in the title. Most titles are published in paperback and as an ebook. Paperbacks are available in traditional bookshops. Both print and ebook formats are available online.

Find more titles and sign up to our readers' newsletter
www.collectiveinkbooks.com/paganism

You Tube

For video content, author interviews and more, please subscribe to our YouTube channel.

MoonBooksPublishing

Follow us on social media for book news, promotions and more:

Facebook: Moon Books

Instagram: @MoonBooksCI

X: @MoonBooksCI

TikTok: @MoonBooksCI